# SHANGHAI
## Past and Present

I dedicate this book
to the memory of my grandparents,
Henia and Leib Steinberg,
and the families they had both lost
in Rowene during the War.

# SHANGHAI
## Past and Present

**A CONCISE SOCIO-ECONOMIC HISTORY, 1842–2012**

Niv Horesh

**sussex**
ACADEMIC
PRESS
*Brighton • Portland • Toronto*

2 4 6 8 10 9 7 5 3

*First published in hardcover 2014, reprinted in paperback 2015, in Great Britain by*
SUSSEX ACADEMIC PRESS
PO Box 139
Eastbourne BN24 9BP


*Distributed in North America by*
SUSSEX ACADEMIC PRESS
ISBS Publisher Services
920 NE 58th Ave #300, Portland, OR 97213, USA

*British Library Cataloguing in Publication Data*
A CIP catalogue record for this book is available from the British Library.


*Library of Congress Cataloging-in-Publication Data*
Horesh, Niv.
Shanghai, past and present : a concise socio-economic history, 1842–2012 / Niv Horesh.
pages   cm.
Includes bibliographical references and index.
ISBN 978-1-84519-631-8 (hardcover : alkaline paper)
ISBN 978-1-84519-699-8 (paperback : alkaline paper)
    1. Shanghai (China)—Economic conditions. 2. Shanghai (China)—Social conditions. I. Title.
HC428.S47H67  2014
330.951'132—dc23

2013048547

Typeset and designed by Sussex Academic Press, Brighton & Eastbourne.
Printed by TJ International, Padstow, Cornwall.

# Contents

# Preface

Does Shanghai really need another book to sing its praise and retell its well-known history ? Surprisingly, the answer might turn out to be 'yes' because a *comprehensive* economic history of the city bringing the narrative up to the present has not yet been attempted in English. What is more, those *well-known* facts (or factoids) about the city have been sensationalised ad nauseam in popular literature, thus perhaps overshadowing many valid questions about Shanghai's ascendancy that are of a more academic nature. A few exceptions do exist, though by and large a nuanced account of how modern Shanghai rose to fame, and how by comparison it meshed with the pre-modern Chinese economy in the millennium prior, is much needed.

To write a *comprehensive* history of a complex city such as Shanghai would involve a substantial collaborative archival effort. But surprisingly, to the best of my knowledge not even a *concise* economic history of the city has been attempted by Western academics. The volume at hand addresses this lacuna, whilst sparing readers tracts of history that are already well-covered in the academic and popular literature, e.g. the 1870s–1900s, or the mid-940s. In other words, this book is *not* a chronologically-framed primer marginally adding to a huge body of work on the city's past, but an attempt to grab readers' and scholars' attention to arguably lesser-known aspects of the city's evolution and to seldom-raised questions.

For these reasons, the book does not purport to draw exhaustively on all Shanghai titles by previous generations of historians. Indeed many writers I hold in high regard, e.g. Ding Richu, are not cited simply because I aim to focus on novel issues. Throughout, I have implicitly approached my chosen topics through the prism of New Institutional Economics (NIE), and with a desire to place Shanghai's evolution in as broad a global perspective as possible.

NIE suggests, contrary to neo-classical economic theory, that happenstance as well as historic precedent can very often determine economic outcomes. As economic settings are conditioned by past choices, there can be no one-size-fits-all formula for urban economic success. Yet, what it takes to appreciate Shanghai's story is not just theory but an understanding of how other metropolises rose to prominence around the world. Examination of the complex social and cultural identity formed in the city since 1842 can only enrich one's understanding of the city's economic setting – I would venture to say – even if neo-classical theory wholly discounts culture as a determinant of economic outcomes.

Shanghai history has become a bit of a cottage industry, such that more novel approaches are now required. This can perhaps be demonstrated by a personal anecdote. My first book, published in 2009, was titled *Shangahi's Bund and Beyond*. At the time I thought I had struck upon a brilliant pun with which to convey the city's distinctiveness from the rest of China. Nevertheless, as I was to discover in my later forays into the city's history, that precise title had already been used aeons beforehand. In 1927, the New York publisher Payson & Clarke released a title by Philip Kerby called *Beyond the Bund*. Therein, Kerby colourfully recounted his adventures sailing around Shanghai, and travelling further inland. Though for obvious reasons our two books are completely different pieces of work, Kerby's had in some way honed in on precisely the same message I would later try to convey in my own title: Shanghai was unique and not to be confused with the rest of China. Needless to say, any vestigial pretence to originality I entertained since 2009 shrivelled upon stumbling over Kerby's rare book in my searches for pre-war Western sources on Shanghai at the British Library.

So the lesson I learnt was that, quite often, "novel" approaches to Shanghai and insights into its history can actually be re-discovered or re-enforced in long forgotten sources, huge as the pertinent literature is. My claim to novelty here does not mean similar ideas had not been raised before somewhere; only that conventional wisdom about Shanghai nowadays might have brushed them aside somewhat. In that sense I am not only indebted to the scholarship of previous generations and to authors whose work did not receive the attention it deserved, but *also* to contemporary Shanghai luminaries who have indirectly or quite literally led me toward many sources and ideas, and whose own rigorous research standards have been inspirational: Mark Elvin (Oxford University), Xiong Yuezhi (Shanghai Academy of Social Sciences), Cheng Linsun (University of Massachusetts), Chiara Betta (School of African and Oriental Studies), Du Xuncheng (Shanghai University of Finance and

Economics), Hong Jiaguan (Shanghai Academy of Social Sciences), Richard Burdekin (Claremont MacKenna College), Robert Bickers (Bristol University), Christian Henriot (Institut d'Asie Orientale), Jeffrey Wasserstrom (University of California), Debin Ma (London School of Economics), Tomoko Shiroyama (Hitotsubashi University), Brian Martin (Australian National University), and Linda Johnson (Michigan State University).

Not a Shanghai aficionado by natural inclination, I would nevertheless like to acknowledge Shanghai residents who have made my stay there over the years all the more pleasant even if they did not succeed in diminishing my preference for Beijing: Ma Jun, Yuqiong (Jade) Qin, and Li Linguo.

Fritz Kuhlman, a true mate, died in Shanghai in 2009 amid tragic circumstances. My sense of life and death in this city is stamped with his big smile and contagious non-conformism.

# 1

# Introduction

# The Shanghai Experience, 1842–2009

To many transient observers Shanghai seemed "incomparable" before World War II. Once foreigners had been allowed to settle in a so-called mudflat opposite the walled "Native City" in 1842, Shanghai developed by leaps and bounds. Immune to Chinese sovereignty, and months away from London by sea, the city acquired a reputation for *laissez-faire* and the mystique of hybridity and vice.[1]

Consider this rather passionate description from a Western tourist guidebook to the city published in 1935:[2]

> Cosmopolitan Shanghai, city of amazing paradoxes and fantastic contrasts; Shanghai the beautiful, bawdy, and gaudy, contradiction of manners and morals; a vast brilliantly-hued cycloramic, panoramic mural of the best and the worst of Orient and Occident. Shanghai, with its modern skyscrapers, the highest buildings in the world outside of the Americas, and its straw huts shoulder high. Modern department stores that pulse with London, Paris, and New York; native emporiums with lacquered ducks and salt eggs, and precious silks and jades, and lingerie and silver, with amazing bursts of advertising colour and more amazing bursts from advertising musicians, compensating with gusto for lack of harmony and rhythm. Modern motors throbbing with the power of eighty horses march abreast with tattered one-man power rickshaws; velveted limousines with silk-clad Chinese multi-millionaires surrounded by Chinese and Russian bodyguards bristling with automatics for protection against the constant menace of kidnapping (foreigners are not molested); Chinese gentlemen in trousers; Chinese gentlemen in satin skirts. Shanghai the bizarre, cinematographic presentation of humanity, its vices and virtues; the City of Blazing

Night; cabarets; Russian and Chinese and Japanese complaisant "dance hostesses"; city of missions and hospitals and brothels. Men of title and internationally notorious fugitives tip cocktails in jovial camaraderie.

This introductory chapter is aimed, nevertheless, at easing non-specialist readers into the warp and weft of Shanghai's modern history by insisting on a less sensationalist comparison of the city's economy in the pre-war era (1842–1937) with its post-war reform thrust following the 1990 designation of Pudong precinct as China's primary financial centre. It will seek to explore why Shanghai was a magnet for so many Chinese entrepreneurs and intellectuals before World War II, as the passage above might indicate; it will then explore whether the reformed makeup of Shanghai in the 21st century can bring about fresh urban dynamism, that might help shake off the post-war legacy of state dirigisme and create a truly global innovation hub. Building on the latest literature in urban development, management and economic history, this chapter will focus on four elements that are conventionally seen as vital to sustaining innovation: well-functioning capital markets, respect for property rights, free information flow and a quality education system. Inevitably, it will leave other important areas of exploration to future research, because these are only associated with the contemporary Chinese economy, e.g. research clustering or fiscal federalism.[3]

The bigger conceptual framework of the comparison drawn here is *practical* in nature because the historical conditions of the pre-war period cannot be perfectly reproduced. Shanghai of the 21st-century cannot be the same as the one of the early 20th century. Therefore, the question to be pursued is not whether it is *desirable* to reproduce the same "urban dynamism" that defined the pre-war era but what can be *learnt* about contemporary Shanghai when we place it in historical perspective.

## Shanghai's Position in the Chinese Pre-War Economy

Assessment of pre-war Shanghai's contribution to the economic modernization of China has been an ongoing academic pursuit but the jury is still out. The rapidly changing political and social circumstances in the People's Republic of China (PRC) often call for a review of past performance in view of present achievements and failures. In the field of Shanghai Studies, such major scholarly reviews can be traced every two decades or so.

For example, in 1981 Marie-Claire Bergère, soon to become the doyenne of Shanghai Development Studies in the West, critiqued Rhoads Murphey whose work had embodied conventional wisdom in the field in the 1950s. In his *Shanghai: Key to Modern China* (1953), Murphey cast pre-war Shanghai as an all-important bridge-head of Western innovation in East Asia against the backdrop of the Communist takeover of the Mainland. By 1977, however, Murphey had come to view pre-war Shanghai's role within the Mainland as a 'fly on an elephant's back'. In other words, Murphey recast pre-war Shanghai as a small enclave of modernity that was ultimately insignificant to the lives of most ordinary Chinese.[4]

Bergère, on the other hand, identified valuable sprouts of civil society, innovation and free enterprise in "golden-age" Shanghai (1920s), when Chinese state power was in decline, but pointed to the resurgence of dirigisme and the stifling of free-markets in the 1930s, after the Nationalists (*Kuomintang* – KMT) had come to power. She suggested that the 1920s saw the birth of a bolder breed of Chinese businessmen, steeped in the internal dynamics of China's rural hinterland, but equally conversant with market conditions around the world.[5]

Chinese intellectuals influenced by radical Western ideology flocked to Shanghai in their thousands in the 1920s. As part of this ferment, the city came to host the founding of the Chinese Communist Party (CCP) in 1921, and was to play a role in the KMT's rise to power nationally in 1927. But ironically, the two rival parties were averse to the free-wheeling nature of the city in the 1920s precisely because both were autocratic.

KMT founder Sun Yat-sen had dreamt of "reforming" Shanghai's wayward character; of subjecting the city's foreign-run precincts straddling Puxi (west of the Huangpu river) to Chinese government control. To that end, he envisioned what was still a boggy and sparsely-populated Pudong district (East of the Huangpu river) as the seat of a new Chinese municipality with strong central powers. After Sun's death, and following its unification of China in 1928, the KMT appointed Wu Tiecheng to accomplish this mission. Wu, who had been educated in Japan, launched grand architectural projects in the 1930s but, overall, because of rampant corruption in their ranks, KMT municipal authorities failed to demonstrate that they were able to manage the Chinese precincts as efficiently as the foreign concession areas.[6]

The success of foreign-run Shanghai cannot be understood accurately enough without considering the plight of the surrounding Chinese pre-war economy as a whole. In the 1980s, economists such as Rawski and Brandt tended to revise conventional Western views of China's pre-war economy as stagnant, tradition-bound and politically-repressed. Rawski and Brandt argued that net annual GDP growth was at approximately 1% between 1842 and 1937, and that Shanghai's modern economy had had a pronounced positive spill-over effect in the hinterland.[7]

Nonetheless, more recent work by younger scholars contends with one of the two main arguments underpinning this revisionist view, providing a more balanced picture. It calls into question the notion that China's pre-war economy enjoyed a higher degree of financial integration than previously thought. Debin Ma, in particular, alludes to the fact that much of Rawski's upbeat assessment of China's overall economic performance hinges on the misapplication of Shanghai's urban growth dynamic and cosmopolitan flair to the rest of the country. The exuberance, entrepreneurship and dynamism of the Shanghanese economy did spill over to the outlying provinces of Jiangsu and Zhejiang but were virtually absent elsewhere in this vast country.[8]

Scholars today seem to agree that pre-war Shanghai, with its semi-colonial setting and its advantageous location as a gateway to the fertile Yangtze Delta, served as an important catalyst for the modernization of the Chinese economy as from 1842. Yet more work is needed to explain operative differences between expatriate-run firms in Shanghai and Chinese businesses in other cities where semi-colonial privileges did not clearly obtain. Needless to say, variegated climates, production relations, geography and factor endowment all significantly account for the dichotomy between Shanghai and China's vast and predominantly rural hinterland. What seems to be lacking in much of the pertinent literature, however, is the epistemology of economic development.

As a rule of thumb, it would probably make sense to stylize semi-colonial treaty-ports like Tianjin or riverside Guangzhou as an extension of Shanghai's pre-war vibrant economy despite obvious differences in climate and factor endowment with the Yangtze Delta. As a large British-administered concession area and foreign financial institutions, Hankou was perhaps integrated into the very same economic system despite being situated much further inland. But nominal and fairly remote treaty-ports like Mengzi (Yunnan), or Chongqing (Sichuan) may provide instructive contrasts to the fast industrializing Yangtze Delta economy. In other words, the demarcation between the Chinese "hinterland" and "treaty-port" economies should be understood not purely in terms of rural backwardness vs. urban sophistication, or in terms of distance from the coast, but also as the degree to which local peasants produced agricultural commodities for world markets (the Yangtze Delta being a case in point), and the degree to which factor agents had recourse to treaty-port finance and extra-territorial protection.

Settlement size also explains why Shanghai was more vital than other treaty-ports that the European powers had carved up along the China coast. By the 1930s, no less than 150,000 expatriates resided in the city side by side with some four million Chinese, bringing with them a plethora of cultures and ideas. They made up about half of the foreign community in China. Notably, the Chinese community itself was highly heterogeneous, with over half relocating from other parts of the country in search of menial employment or opportunity.

Europeans (including White-Russian refugees) made up about a third of the foreign population; the rest were predominantly Japanese. In all, foreigners accounted for about 4% of the city's total population. Today, unofficial estimates put the number of foreigners residing in Shanghai at about 150,000 out of a total of 15 million – the overwhelming majority being overseas Chinese (1%). Proportionately, then, pre-war Shanghai could be said to have been four times more cosmopolitan than early 21st century Shanghai.[9]

The distinct pre-war population makeup was administered by an equally unique tripartite municipal structure: the Chinese precincts ('Native City') strove to catch up with the efficiently-run Anglo-American (or 'International') concession area, while the more "straightforwardly colonialist" French concession area vied with the other two to attract Chinese investment.[10]

Governed by a semi-elected and highly autonomous body called the Shanghai Municipal Council (SMC), the International concession area was more cosmopolitan in nature albeit devoid of meaningful Chinese representation at the helm. Britons accounted for the majority of SMC executives; it also employed American administrators, Sikh policemen, White Russian stewards and had Jews, Germans and Japanese represented on the board. Members of the *Municipalité de la Concession Française de Changhai* were, on the other hand, handpicked by Paris. This administrative multiplicity supported the free flow of information, and exchange of ideas including radical left-wing ideologies imported from Europe by fringe expatriates.

Newspapers appeared in a host of languages: English, French, German, Yiddish, Russian and Japanese. Magazines appeared in a dozens of other European languages.[11] It is also important to recognize the limits of free speech in pre-war Shanghai. The foreign-run SMC partly resisted warlord pressure to crack down on dissenting Chinese publications. Nonetheless, on some occasions the SMC preferred to appease the warlord government in Beijing by bringing Chinese dissidents before the Mixed Court on sedition charges.[12]

This vibrant milieu was enough to attract scores of university teachers and intellectuals to the city during the early-Republican era (1912–1927); they escaped the repression, incompetence and arbitrary violence of warlord-ravaged China for the *relative* freedom of Shanghai, notwithstanding its association with European imperialism and expatriate snobbery. Chinese intellectuals working from Shanghai came to be known as the *haipai* ('Worldly School'), which contrasted with the traditionalists or *jingpai* ('Capital School'). Whilst *jingpai* education clung to Confucian classics, *haipai* education encouraged the acquisition of vocational and English-language skills. With only 1.5% of China's population at any one time, Shanghai accounted for no less than 41 of the 205 institutions of higher education in China in 1949. It boasted some of the country's best universities, such as Fudan and Jiaotong, as well as prestigious colleges run by missionaries such as Aurora and St John's.[13]

The exchange of ideas and intellectual ferment were facilitated by the most modern infrastructure. Shanghai was the first city on the Mainland to develop extensive telecommunications services. In 1871, for example, the Great Northern Telegraph Company of Denmark laid an underwater telegraph cable from Hong Kong to Shanghai, giving the country its first submerged international communications system. In 1907, a local telephone service was introduced and a long-distance service followed in 1923. By 1949, Shanghai had some 85,000 phone lines installed for about 55,000 subscribers. Although subscription was small compared with cities like London, it made up a third of all telephone lines in China at the time.[14]

Similarly, the city's financial sector was one of the most competitive in Asia with domestic institution gradually matching foreign ones in size and efficiency. By 1934, no less then 33 foreign banks operated in the city, whilst in colonial Hong Kong there were only 17 at the time. Moreover, in the pre-war years, Shanghai's securities markets far outweighed Hong Kong's.[15]

In fact, as Wong Siu-lun has observed, Shanghai was "head and shoulder" above Hong Kong as a metropolis in many other respects during the pre-war era. The tripartite municipal setting in Shanghai yielded quite a different streak of entrepreneurship than the one prevalent in the full-fledged Crown Colony. In Hong Kong, exclusion of Chinese from civil service fostered grass-roots idealization of small-business ownership (*dang laoban*), resulting in a two-tier economy with desultory family-based firms and subcontracting networks running side by side with British multinationals. In Shanghai, on the other hand, the Nationalist takeover of Chinese precincts in 1927 meant that Chinese businesses became increasingly enmeshed with government bureaucracy to the extent that corporatism and salaried employment were the grass-roots ideal. As a result Chinese-run firms could eventually rival the size and scope of multinationals with state backing.[16]

Arguably, the heavy hand of KMT government, its arbitrary tax extraction and co-optation of successful Chinese businesses, explains why, despite Shanghai's preeminence as China's financial center in the pre-war era, the city's stock market remained largely confined to the foreign concession areas. There, independent shareholder rights were much more clearly framed than in the city's Chinese precincts. Yet consular regulators were suspicious of Chinese-owned businesses wishing to incorporate under foreign company law and issue stock. Consequently, the stock market was dominated by foreign-run municipal utilities, trading companies and banks like HSBC. It attracted ethnic Chinese investment *en masse*, but listed very few Chinese industrial ventures. The parallel Chinese-run securities market was, on the other hand, dominated by KMT-issued bonds, effectively crowding out private equity.

There was, in that sense, a striking difference between the Japanese and Chinese securities markets before the turn of the last century. Whereas Japanese securities markets helped finance the buildup of a nationwide railway network and seminal industry, China's was heavily weighted toward foreign banking and insurance companies, as well as municipal utilities with little interest in expanding their services outside the city perimeters. In the 1870s, railways were being built in both China and Japan, but Japan achieved a commanding lead within three decades in absolute railway mileage and, of course, in terms of the ratio of mileage to population. Until 1890, two systems of railways operated in Japan side by side: a government-owned one and, equally importantly, one operated by joint-stock companies able to mobilize funds on domestic securities markets. For the impoverished early-Meiji government to defray the construction of the whole railway network would have been fiscally prohibitive. In that sense, joint-stock finance was crucial to Japan's early modernization effort.

The late-imperial Chinese court preferred, on balance, to borrow overseas at a higher cost, and contract railway construction out to foreign firms if only to avert the onset of private enterprise. Then the KMT spurned overseas credit in favor of floating public debt domestically, but was equally suspicious of non-aligned private enterprises. By 1931, it was also embroiled in campaigns against Japanese Kanto army, which invaded Manchuria, and against the Chinese Communist Party (CCP)-held rural enclaves. Thus, on the eve of World War II, Shanghai's foreign concessions boasted one of the most advanced tramline systems in the world, while China's railway network was woefully inadequate.[17]

In conclusion, Shanghai in the pre-war era seemed to have attracted Westerners because it provided easy and secure access to China's wealthiest provinces, while retaining a distinct *laissez-faire* environment. Chinese intellectuals and investors, for their part, appear to have continually converged on Shanghai *not* because the semi-colonial legal system necessarily protected civil liberties or press freedom, *but* because its *laissez-faire* environment probably minimized the perceived risks of Chinese government usurpation. That said, the city's competitive tripartite structure meant some Chinese firms enjoyed state backing in KMT-run precincts, grew in size and eventually rivaled multinationals.

## Post-War Shanghai: Central Planning and Reform

The Communist unification of Mainland China in 1949 augured a drastic makeover of Shanghai's role as an Asian if not a global financial hub. The city had been portrayed as a mainspring of KMT corruption and bourgeois degradation in CCP propaganda but, nonetheless, it still harbored China's industrial base and a wealth of intellectual resources and could not be easily dispensed with. In its first three years in power, the CCP wisely adopted a moderate platform that allowed for the retention of some private enterprise and a deliberate transfer of urban management skills to party bureaucrats, who were mostly from rural backgrounds.

The city had been affected by an exodus of wealthy industrialists on the eve of KMT retreat in 1948. Most chose to move to Hong Kong in fear of communist reprisal. This was compounded in the early 1950s by the CCP's decision to relocate many factories further inland as part of a strategy to make China less vulnerable to coastal invasion. Then during the 1960s and 1970s, Shanghai's image as a bastion of bourgeois liberalism was turned on its head, as it became a rallying point for Maoist zealotry. But, contrary to popular perceptions, the city's share of the national economy actually rebounded from the industrial dispersion of the 1950s.[18]

Inherently prone to manipulation, Chinese government statistics can nevertheless draw out the complex post-war trend: Shanghai's annual industrial output grew by 24.9% on average during the deliberate transition period to communist central planning (1949–52). This was still a lower rate than the national average (34.81%) at the time, reflecting the CCP's massive industrial build-up in, and factory relocation to, the hinterland. Notably, during much of Mao's febrile Cultural Revolution era (1965–1970), the gap between annual industrial output growth in Shanghai and the rest of China actually narrowed down to 10% vs. 11.7% respectively. More counterintuitive still is the fact that through much of the Great Leap Forward (1957–1965), an era often associated with anti-urban rhetoric, Shanghai's annual industrial output growth (9.84%) actually exceeded the rest of China (8.9%).[19]

The post-war era also ushered in much tighter population control measures in the city. Between 1949 and 1976, the CCP implemented a number of large-scale outward migration programmes, which compounded the already acute shortages of skilled laborers and technicians that had ensued from the exodus of Chinese businessmen to Hong Kong, the departure of the city's foreign community, and the relocation of many factories to the hinterland.[20]

These figures, however, reveal only part of the CCP agenda. The party did not seek to eliminate Shanghai's economy but to "socialize" it. In other words, the CCP had attempted at first to extract whatever it could from whatever private wealth that remained there in 1949. It then gingerly nationalized private enterprise, and as of 1952 relocated much of the city's manufacturing base elsewhere. Whilst Shanghai's industry in the pre-war era was overwhelming light in nature (mainly textiles), the city was to become during the first five-year plan (1952–1957) a center for heavy industry in line with the party's overall emphasis on metallurgy and petrochemical capacity building at the expense of consumer goods. However, the overall result of this top-down shift from light to heavy industry was such that by 1977 Shanghai accounted for only 14% of China's industrial output, compared with almost 33% in the pre-war era.[21]

Chinese light industry as a whole recovered only in the late 1970s, as Deng Xiaoping – China's new helmsman – re-opened the country to foreign investment, and as scores of labor-intensive assembly lines were set up by offshore firms across the border from Hong Kong. Arguably because of its pre-war legacy, Deng was reluctant to open Shanghai up for foreign investment during the first decade of the reform era (1978–1988), preferring instead the then more peripheral fishing village of Shenzhen, because of the latter's proximity to bustling Hong Kong.[22]

In 1991, Deng Xiaoping changed course. Keen to demonstrate to the rest of the world that China could avert pressure by CCP conservatives to fold back economic reform following the Tianan'men student movement, Deng visited Shenzhen to embolden local cadres. Equally important, he approved new preferential-tax development zones for foreign investment in Greater Shanghai, and allowed the redevelopment of Pudong – first envisioned by Sun Yat-sen in 1921 – to go ahead.

Shanghai has since attracted key foreign manufacturing plants including that of German automaker Volkswagen, but its share of China's industrial output has not significantly rebounded, because development zones are now spread more evenly across China's eastern seaboard. Whilst its share of China's population has remained fairly stable since the late 1970s (around 1.2%), its share of China's GDP had actually dropped from 6.91% in 1978 to 4.38% in 1994.[23] The government-led redevelopment of Pudong had immediately transformed the city's skyline in the early 1990s, but commensurate structural change to the economy did not seem to follow. In 1994, for example, the private sector accounted for only 2.8% of the city's workforce compared with 9.8% in Guangzhou.[24]

Official PRC statistics for the 2000s suggest that the Yangtze Delta is gradually catching up with the Pearl River Delta

(Guangdong province), where Shenzhen and Guangzhou are situated, and where Deng's reforms started in 1979. However, in contrast to the pre-war years, growth in the Yangtze Delta spills over more significantly across Jiangsu and Zhejiang. While Shanghai is still an important node of finance to this region – as a self-governing city with limited land reserve – it still accounted for only 4.5% of China's GDP in 2006. [25]

Shanghai staked its claim to fame through both the pre-war and post-war reform eras primarily as a financial hub. It is therefore crucial to understand the structural differences that set these eras apart, if one is to venture a guess about China's future. As indicated above, before World War II, China's main securities market was run by Shanghai expatriates and governed by British colonial corporate law. It was mainly geared toward foreign-run financial institutions and municipal utilities. A significant departure from the pre-war pattern is the fact that China's securities markets no longer gravitate toward Shanghai alone. Symbolically, the first stock exchange to be opened in the reform era was set up in Shenzhen in June 1990. In November that year, the Shanghai stock exchange was re-established after a 38-year hiatus. Today, China's securities market is fairly evenly divided between Shanghai and Shenzhen, and is invariably geared toward state-owned industrial behemoths. Realistically capitalized at US$ 0.5 trillion, this securities market is nominally the third-largest in Asia (after Tokyo and Hong Kong), but only about a third of its listed equity is tradable, and merely a fourth of the firms listed are privately-run. [26]

That said, the relative paucity of privately-run publicly-listed firms is a red thread linking the pre and post-war periods; it is an issue that is clearly relevant to the nature of China's modernization effort in the long-haul, as Bowen and Rose have argued.[27] After almost three decades of reform in the PRC, private enterprise and private property rights are still lamely-framed within the legal system. Re-established with much fanfare in 1990, the Shanghai and Shenzhen domestic bourses rarely float private firms; PRC taxation policy and the predominantly state-owned banking system similarly disadvantage private small and medium size enterprises (SMEs) without intimate political connections in favor of well-networked government-backed ventures and foreign firms.[28]

Courts in the PRC are reluctant to adjudicate litigation of accounting fraud, enforce minority shareholder rights, or penalize corporate intransparency. This is because the government is often a majority stakeholder in the forms sued. Provincial authorities similarly exert pressure on its judiciary when investors from other parts of China bring charges against local firms. But arguably most pernicious is the Chinese securities market's stochastic nature. In 1996, for example, 57% of US corporate stock moved in the same direction. In post-Communist Poland the figure was 82%. In China, virtually the entire market (91.3%) moved along to the same beat that year. This suggest cycles rather than specific company performance inform share prices, and elicits the skepticism with which investors view the data Chinese listed companies put out.[29]

Another stark difference between the pre- and post-war periods lies in the area of logistics and infrastructure. Once strung along the silted Bund, Shanghai's pre-war port nevertheless handled almost half of Mainland China's maritime traffic and foreign trade. Container facilities had since been expanded and moved closer ashore, but the city's port had often came in for criticism in the 1990s for falling well short of Hong Kong and Singapore.

By 2006, however, China boasted no less than 200 seaports, which handled together 3.4 billion tones of goods, up from just 483 million in 1990. Shanghai's newly-developed port, while still one of the largest in China in 2004, was at the time relatively shallow and therefore inaccessible to super-size freighters. That problem was solved only in 2006 with the opening of supplementary deep-water facilities (*Yangshan gang*) not far from Zhoushan island, which are connected to mainland Shanghai by the 32.5 km-long Donghai bridge. Today, with the completion of these facilities, Shanghai has finally become the busiest container port in the world.[30]

Since 1990, capital works were far from confined to port facilities. By 1995, a new water plant, gas works, power plant, sewage facilities and an advanced telecommunications network had been installed in Pudong. The second phase of build-up began in 1996 to the tune of billions of Renminbi (RMB). It saw the construction of the city's second international airport, new subway and tram lines, and a ring-road to alleviate traffic congestion.[31]

In 1985, there was only one phone for every 70 people in Shanghai; 15 years later, more than 97 per cent of the city's residents had a phone installed in their home. By the beginning of 2004, the city had more than 11 million mobile phone subscribers, and 4.3 million internet users. Foreign firms such as Alcatel, McCaw and AT&T were persuaded to enter the market with promises of local-government protection. These companies brought valuable knowhow that helped the municipal authorities tout Shanghai as a 21st-century cyber-hub.[32]

Yet today, in contrast to what one might expect in any Western metropolis, the municipal authorities are not only regulating the telecommunications industry or maintaining infrastructure, but also own the largest ISP and local-content portal (Eastday.com) as well as a string of browser cafés. This degree of local-government permeation of the hi-tech sector seems unique even compared to other PRC cities. Beijing and Guangzhou, for example, have not sought to steer residents to municipally-owned websites in quite the same way.[33]

During Jiang Zemin's decade in power (1993–2003), Shanghai was often seen as the subject of favorable discrimination by the central government, because Jiang and many of his protégés had held posts in the municipal bureaucracy there prior to their elevation on the national scene. The central and local governments provided tax incentives, research funding and venture capital for entrepreneurs willing to bring their expertise to these zones. These efforts were made in conjunction with the local prestigious universities of Fudan and Jiaotong. They have yielded many hardware, software, security, biotech and pharmaceutical ventures, and attracted considerable investment from the likes of Intel, Microsoft and Dell – companies which rarely invest in R&D outside their US home base. Yet anecdotal evidence suggests that the great bulk of R&D activity and start-up initiatives in Shanghai still stem from public funding, and it is unclear how much of it is self-sustaining.[34] What is more, none of the best known homegrown hi-tech companies that have emerged in the PRC to date – Lenovo (Shenzhen), Huawei (Shenzhen), Galanz (Shenzhen), Haier (Qingdao), Baidu (Beijing) – are based in Shanghai or the Yangtze Delta for that matter.

## Afterthoughts

Can this introductory chapter of Shanghai development history be of any interest to contemporary China watchers? With so much attention devoted to themes of Asian economic and political submission in the post-colonial discourse, it is hardly surprising that few attempts have been made to uncover the vibrant legacy of Shanghainese entrepreneurship in the pre-war era, and how it may have presaged China's resurgence in the 21st century. Yet, the resemblance between Shanghai's bustling pre-war concession areas and the Deng-inspired Special Economic Zone model of the 1990s is clear. Both were heavily dependent on external capital flow, preferential treatment of foreign firms and a degree of immunity to central government directives.

The year 1937 signaled the impending implosion of European hegemony in East Asia (with the exception of Hong Kong and Macao) and, in this sense, it is a landmark in the history of Shanghai. Arguably, Shanghai before 1937 was part of the transnational construct of imperialism, and its development had everything to do with the status of a semi-colonial city. The city's international standing and economic accomplishment drew on the infrastructural and cultural connections with the imperial metropolises. By contrast, post-war planning aimed at balancing the demands of nation-building, national integration and – in recent times – of internationalization. As a result, contemporary Shanghai is following a different development formula to the one prescribed in the pre-war era.

How sustainable is this Deng-inspired formula? Little systematic research has been done to that effect, but suggestive analogies between the past and present cannot be completely avoided even as we recognize the significant differences between the two periods. Following China's entry to the World Trade Organisation (WTO), some of the very same foreign banks, which had flourished on the Bund before World War II have once again been authorized to operate in local currency. There are now over 108 foreign banks operating in Shanghai, but unlike the pre-war era, foreign financial institutions play a very small role in the domestic economy (approximately 1.2% in 2002).[35] What remains to be seen is how this *démarche* will project on China's historically ramshackle securities markets and on its brittle private sector. Sociologists might also wonder whether a civil society will ever emerge in China along western lines, but this question is beyond the scope of the present work.

If history is anything to go by, we can expect tough competition as well as convergence between local and foreign banks. As re-entrants to a long-lost market, foreign financial institutions may now be keener than ever to bankroll promising Chinese private ventures that state-owned banks routinely shut out; but whether in the absence of pervasive political reform Shanghai's stock exchange can grow out of its current doldrums, or eventually outshine that of Hong Kong, is doubtful. A counterintuitive (read: ahistorical) solution to this question may ultimately force theorists to consider the emergence of a new 'Capitalism with Chinese characteristics'.

What this introduction might bear out quite concretely is the fact that pre-war Shanghai accounted for a much larger share of China's economy than present-day Shanghai does. Though replete with semi-colonial racialism, and constricted by smaller concessionary boundaries – pre-war Shanghai provided and enhanced a cosmopolitan, individualistic and captivating urban space. It was a place where a Chinese public sphere of sorts was beginning to emerge before 1928. But dirigisme has since been the rule, be it under KMT or CCP aegis. It is state-led development and bureaucratic co-optation of private enterprise that spawned Pudong's impressive yet anodyne skyline. The chapters to follow will unfurl the canvass further in a bid to offer an understanding of Shanghai's economic history that can underpin a more informed debate about its future prospects.

## Notes

1 Barber (1979), pp. 144–159; Bergère (2002), pp. 359–362.
2 *All About Shanghai* (1935), Chapter 6.
3 On these elements of the current reform thrust see, e.g, Qian (2002); Huang (2008).
4 Murphey (1953); Murphey (1977).
5 Bergère (1981), pp. 32–34.
6 Wakeman (1995); cf. MacPherson (1996), pp. 502, 507–508, 514.
7 Rawski (1989); Brandt (1989).
8 See Ma (2008); since Ma shows Shanghai was dependent on hinterland demand for industrial goods, raw material and labour supply, Murphey's (1977) assessment of Shanghai as an inconsequential enclave is further called into question.
9 Ma (2001).
10 Wasserstrom (2000), p. 193.
11 On Shanghai's immense pre-war foreign-language, see e.g. King (1965); Reed (2004); Mittler (2004).
12 Bergère (1981), p. 12.
13 Mak et al. (1996), pp. 377–378.
14 Harwit (2005), p. 1840.
15 Kuilman (2007), p. 28.
16 Wong (1996), pp. 26, 33–34.
17 Cf. Minami (1994); Nobutaka (1954); Noda (1980).

18  Cheung (1996), pp. 56–58.
19  Howe (1981), p. 157 [table 6.2], 159.
20  Wong (1996), pp. 37–40.
21  Compare Ma (2008) with Howe (1981), pp. 167–168, 175–7.
22  Mao and Higano (1996), p. 157.
23  Yeung (1996), table 1.1, p. 15.
24  Cheung (1996), pp. 50–54.
25  Economist Intelligence Unit (2008), pp. 37–38.
26  Chen (2006), pp. 21–22.
27  Bowen and Rose (1998); cf. volume edited by Oi and Walder (1999).
28  Huang (2008).
29  Chen (2006), pp. 33–38.
30  Economist Intelligence Unit (2008), p. 27.
31  Lai et al. (2005), p 305.
32  Harwit (2005), pp. 1837–45.
33  Harwit (2005), pp. 1853–55.
34  Lai et al. (2005), p. 279.
35  Kuilman (2007), pp. 21, 31–33. The old stock exchanges were shut down decisively in 1952 after the transitional period of CCP tolerance of private enterprise.

# 2

# Mystique, Answers and Unanswered Questions

Since its establishment as a treaty-port in 1842 and roughly until the Japanese invasion of China proper in 1937, Shanghai had gradually acquired a reputation as Asia's most spell-binding, entrepreneurial and free-wheeling cities. Interest in the city's pre-war legacy has increased in recent years as a result of the PRC's breakneck economic reform, and the opening up of its archives to foreign scholars. Western academics have begun engaging with these newly-declassified materials in ways that often reshape our understanding of Chinese modern history. Yet the development path that made Shanghai so vital to what may be loosely defined as 'Chinese modernity' has scarcely been agreed on.

One of many testaments to Shanghai's enduring appeal is the 2006 CBC television documentary *Legendary Cities of Sin*, in which it is portrayed as a megalopolis that was on par with Paris and Berlin between the two world wars. Shanghai's mystique is an even more potent drawcard in the realm of cinema with scores of Hollywood and Chinese productions set in the pre-Communist era – Ang Lee's most recent feature film *Lust, Caution* (2007) being just one, fairly obvious example. In the realm of Western scholarship, Shanghai's significance to understanding early-modern China is borne out by an explosion of historic surveys and research guide publications, of which Jeffrey Wasserstrom's *Global Shanghai* and Ulrich Menzel's online *Sytematische Bibliographie* are perhaps the most useful.[1] Other important resources on the city's past include the illuminating *Tales of Old China*, a website managed by the Chinese Economic Review Publishing Company with contributions from a number of Western Shanghai scholars; *Virtual Shanghai*, a blog edited by Professor Christian Henriot featuring original documents, old maps and photos of the city; and the AHRC-funded Chinese Maritime

Customs Project, run by Bristol University in conjunction with the Second Historical Archive in Nanjing.

The academic interest in the West is quite naturally outweighed by Chinese scholars' output. Scores of new history theses, articles and monographs in Chinese draw on material from the Shanghai Municipal Archives. A fair few even venture a somewhat more 'benign' picture of the city's capitalistic legacy than was the case until the 1990s, as if to thereby vindicate its contemporary association with foreign investment.[2] But party-state tutelage of social science and modern history research institutes hems in the latitude of explicitly novel approaches. The result is a body of work that, while often laden with previously unavailable primary-source data, is not necessarily bound by consistent analytical focus.[3]

This is not to say that Chinese and foreign Shanghai historians do not engage ecumenically. There are already a number of platforms where ideas, theoretical concepts and research outcomes flow in both directions, even if cross-pollination is harder to discern in published work. Translated articles on Shanghai by Chinese historians appear regularly in journals such as *Chinese Studies in History* or the *Journal of Modern Chinese History*. Similarly, surveys of Western scholarship on Chinese urban history appear on occasion in PRC volumes.[4]

As noted above, for Western and Chinese scholars alike, an important milestone was access granted to the Shanghai Municipal Archive pre-war repository as of the 1990s. The sheer volume and diversity of historic material available there has already led to revisionist narratives of, for example, the vitality of Chinese financiers in Shanghai in the face of what was – and for the most part is still – conventionally seen as the KMT's autocracy and extortion of Chinese business elite.[5] In PRC publications, readers do come across more hard evidence and a little less lip service to Marxism-Leninism than was found in standard compilations like Tang Zhenchang's until not long ago.[6]

In this chapter, we expound in the main on a number of Western studies of pre-war Shanghai because of their influential theoretical framework and robust primary-source evidence, but do not gloss over lesser-known yet no less robust studies in Chinese and Japanese that have advanced our knowledge of the city a great deal. Plainly put, the following passages will attempt to extract the pertinent literature into discursive threads that may help better explain what made pre-war Shanghai 'tick', and clarify the analytical framework of this book as well how it might contribute to the existing academic and popular literature on the city.

Our aims here are to explore whether the city's phenomenal growth after 1842 was essentially due to endogenous or exogenous factors; whether its foreign-introduced legal system substantively contributed to Chinese enterprise or the emergence of a Chinese 'public sphere'; whether KMT-administered Shanghai out- or under-performed the city's foreign concessions; how integrated has Shanghai been with the rest of China or other Asian financial hubs; and how enmeshed were the city's sub-ethnicities within themselves. Finally, we shall try to underscore the relevance of the pre-war era to 21st-century Shanghai.

## 'Chinese' or 'Foreign' Development Formula?

Arguably, the most intellectually stimulating new trend in Shanghai Studies in the West has been that which challenges the overriding significance of Western colonial stimuli to Shanghai's development pattern. Contrary to Fairbank's famous 'foreign impact – Chinese reaction' paradigm, scholars like Lu and Johnson search the root cause for Shanghai's dynamism in a late-Imperial social and economic transformation of the Lower Yangtze Delta (Jiangnan) that had begun well before British gunboats opened up the region for trade.[7]

Theirs is an approach somewhat reminiscent of Paul Cohen's call for more emphasis on Chinese agency in Western historiography, and perhaps suggestive of Chakrabarty's later preoccupation with provincialising the European historic experience.[8] Lu in particular argues that Shanghai's Chinese petty urbanites (*xiao shimin*), who made the bulk of the city's population, had clung to traditional rather than imported lifestyles. They bought fresh groceries daily from ubiquitous peddlers; they observed Chinese festivities with gusto but kept aloof when foreigners marked Christmas and New Year's Eve in the city; they had their nightsoil unceremoniously collected just like their peasant relatives in the hinterland; they invariably preferred rustic cuisine to 'fancy' Western dishes (*da can*); and they lived in distinct atomized neigbourhoods (*lilong*), whose hybrid architecture featured novel imported *motifs* like arched stone masonry or balconies but owed every bit as much to traditional Chinese imagery.[9]

For Lu, the most important factor in the growth and subsequent economic take-off of Shanghai was not Western-designed institutions but endogenous dynamics. He explains that the concession area which the British had carved up a few kilometres north of the old walled city remained a desultory, segregated backwater between 1842 and 1853. Then the Small Sword (*xiao dao*) uprising against the provincial Qing authorities (1853), and later the mayhem unleashed by the Taiping rebellion in Jiangnan (1860–62), drove thousands of wealthy Chinese to take refuge in the small British settlement. Under pressure from British landowners raring for a windfall, the British consul in Shanghai allowed these refugees to rent hastily-built housing, paving the way for Sino-foreign cohabitation with the half-hearted acquiescence of the local imperial superintendent (*daotai* or Taotai as this position was known to Westerners).

Ultimately, one might therefore assume, it was the booming realty market amid revolts and declining imperial powers – *not* Western semi-colonial tutelage – that secured the settlement's prosperity for decades to come. All things being equal, this is a cogent proposition that has to be examined in conjunction with the line of argumentation advanced by Linda Johnson.

Published four years prior to Lu's, Johnson's book set out to refute the colonialist myth that Shanghai had been an insignificant fishing village before the British settled there in 1842. Drawing mainly on imperial district gazetteers, she shows that the city had been a major commercial port as early as the 13th century; and that by the early 19th century it was among the twenty largest cities in China. Though not entirely unknown to specialists, these are in and of themselves important facts in the storyline that complement Lu's account. Indeed, as Kerrie MacPherson reminds us, unlike Japan's two great ports of Yokohama and Kobe, which rose to prominence only after the opening of Japan to foreign trade in the 1850s, Shanghai's walled city had already been an important regional port in the 17th century.[10]

Both Lu and Johnson offer a carefully-constructed bottom-up narrative that is closely attuned to demographic flows and to the underlying regional traditions of Jiangnan, but is somewhat dismissive of the exponential growth in trade volumes and financial-sector services, and of the permeation of Western-style municipal services, missionary-run hospitals, mass media and entertainment after 1842.[11] Leo Ou-Fan Lee and Lynn Pan, by comparison, present a nuanced portrayal in their respective studies of Shanghai's "new" urban culture in the inter-war period and during 1930s, stressing that while it was mostly wealthy Chinese and intellectuals who patronized Shanghai's many coffee-houses, large plebeian Chinese crowds were attracted to Western-style theatres, dancing halls, horse racing, and department stores.[12]

Notably, there is one point where Lu and Johnson's accounts clearly differ. Drawing out his sketch of *lilong* life, Lu observes that these pre-war urban communities had lacked anything like the civic spirit embodied in, for example, coeval Tokyo through neighbourhood committees (Japanese: *chōkai*). Johnson, on the other hand, is convinced that the seeds of an early-modern Chinese "public space" had already been manifest in Jiangnan charitable gentry mobilization well before 1842.[13]

This point of difference echoes a much larger debate that unfolded in the 1990s, particularly among American scholars, on the absence or emergence of a Habermasian 'public sphere' and 'civil society' in early-modern Chinese cities, that is, the onset of venues for discussion of current affairs and autonomous public mobilization beyond imperially-prescribed mouthpieces or bureaucratic sanction.[14] In his rebuttal of the utility of the concept of 'public sphere' within the broad sweep of Chinese urban history, Frederic Wakeman made a clear distinction between Shanghai and other treaty-ports along the China coast, and between Shanghai and miasmic Beijing where the foreign presence was much smaller: no other Chinese city but semi-colonial Shanghai could develop anything tantamount to a 'public sphere', because only in Shanghai was free press allowed to operate.[15]

Wakeman's argument about Shanghai's exceptionalism is implicitly supported by Rudolf Wagner, who posits that the vitality of the city in the pre-war era cannot be understood without paying attention to Chinese-language publications like the ubiquitous *Shenbao*. This newspaper was a popular outlet for market data, bulky consumer advertising as well as polemics on current affairs in the city and China beyond; it had actually been set up in 1872 by an English entrepreneur, Ernest Major, who astutely recognized the absence of such a medium as a daily newspaper in China. Major's brainchild was sold off to Chinese investors in 1908, but *Shenbao* continued to report on controversial issues and its circulation rapidly grew thereafter.[16]

Pointing to the subtle means by which a foreign-introduced

medium like S*henbao* could stimulate the mindset of Shanghai urbanites and reach across to other Chinese treaty-port audiences, Wagner later levelled criticism – in an online review – at Christopher Reed's award-winning study of Shanghai 'print capitalism'.[17] This was precisely because Wagner thought Reed had not sufficiently explored the foreign roots of the industry and their implications; *Shenbao* was comparatively staid in its editorial tone but it catalysed the establishment of other Chinese-language publications that openly challenged imperial orthodoxy and lampooned court corruption, as Ye Xiaoqing and Wang Juan's recent studies both show.[18]

Wagner's lifelong interest in the Chinese-language press opened up an important intellectual vista, inspiring an immense body of work that explores complex themes ranging from the tenor of tabloid satire to the semiotics of the Sino-Foreign encounter. But the unabated proliferation of studies on print media in the city also begs the question whether they might not ultimately belabour the argument, considering that authoritative studies by Nicholas Clifford and Robert Bickers clearly show that foreign-administered Shanghai often repressed free speech; that it was racially regimented if not explicitly racist, and effectively devoid of representative government.[19]

Most specialist readers would be aware, for example, that there were virtually no Chinese in executive positions either at the International or French municipal councils which ran the foreign concession areas despite the fact that Chinese contributed the bulk of their revenue; Chinese were excluded from upmarket social venues through much of the pre-war era; marriage between Europeans and "Asiatics" was formally discouraged. And Chinese firms could *not* incorporate locally without appointing foreign nationals to chair their boards.

In that sense, there might be a risk that non-specialist readers could erroneously associate the academic preoccupation in the West with the 'free press' underpinnings of pre-war Shanghai with sentiments that white residents of the city ('Shanghailanders') had themselves entertained. Shanghailanders believed theirs was an enlightened 'model settlement' where free speech thrived. It was seen as neither part of Asia nor answerable to Westminister.[20] On the other hand, there must have been something qualitatively different about foreign-run Shanghai that eventually made it rise to prominence above all the other four treaty-ports opened to British trade in 1842. After all, Guangzhou (Canton) had been established as a Sino-Foreign maritime entrepôt long before; Xiamen (Amoy) was an important outlet of tea exports; Fuzhou had an elaborate moneyshop system; Ningbo was centrally located and offered convenient deep-water access.[21]

Either way, the famous *Subao* case of 1903 clearly shows the limit of free speech in the city's foreign concession areas. Established in 1896 and registered in the Japanese consulate, *Subao* was the first among many Shanghai newspapers that criticized Qing officialdom. In 1902, under the editorship of Zou Rong, *Subao* called for the violent overthrow of the Qing. Aghast, the Viceroy of Zhejiang and Jiangsu, Wei Guangtao, dispatched envoys to persuade the predominantly British-run Shanghai Municipal Council (SMC) to have the newspaper muzzled. Consequently, the British-run Shanghai Municipal Police (SMP) arrested six editorial staff members including Zou, who was sentenced to three-year imprisonment.[22]

Notably, the SMP declined the request for Zou's extradition by the Qing government because it feared such a measure would compromise extra-territoriality. In that sense, the adjudication of the *Subao* case and the fate of the defendants was much better than the fate of many other dissidents residing elsewhere in China. More significantly, numerous reports concerning the trial appeared at the time in the local press, thereby advancing perhaps the understanding of Western legal precepts by the city's Chinese elite.

But the persecution of journalists and labour activists intensified during the 1920s. This time of course the target was not anti-Manchu but "Bolshevized" literature.[23] Indeed, it would be hard to understand the vehemence with which Chinese – petty urbanites, students, intellectuals, labour activists and even KMT rightists – attacked the foreign grip on Shanghai from its very inception without reference to the plutocratic nature of the city's municipal governance.

## The Legal Framework

The degree to which relative press freedom in Shanghai qualitatively transformed Chinese political consciousness cannot be effectively examined without consideration of the complex legal system that evolved in the city at large. During the pre-war era, Shanghai was divided into three administrative zones: the international concession area or 'Anglo-American' settlement (run by the highly autonomous SMC); the French Concession area (popularly known as 'Frenchtown') which was much more amenable to Paris; the walled city and its environs (known interchangeably as the 'Native City', the 'Chinese City', 'Nantao' or more formally as Nanshi), which were administered by the imperial *daotai*, and after 1912, by warlord and KMT functionaries.

While Chinese legal precepts obtained in Nanshi, the Qing reluctantly recognized the foreign settlements as "extra-territorial". This meant in practice that Westerners residing in the city were immune to prosecution by Chinese officials: they could only be tried by magistrates at their respective consulates. Cases where both foreign and Chinese residents were implicated were brought before the 'Mixed Court' (*huishen gongxie*), where Chinese magistrates sat right from inception, but where Western Assessors eventually wrested control of the proceedings.

Debin Ma has recently suggested that Western jurisprudence – of which press freedom was presumably a derivative but with corporate law and individual property rights at its heart – might explain more than any other factor Shanghai's economic vibrancy.[24] Ma's pioneering quantitative work points to a critically under-studied aspect of pre-war Shanghai: while we already have excellent macro-level studies of consumer culture, labour activism, native-place bonds and organized crime – the institutional underpinnings of the foreign settlements and their projection on to quotidian transactions are not yet entirely clear.[25] Perhaps now that the Shanghai Municipal Archives have been electronically catalogued it is time to re-examine with hard documentary evidence how 'extra-territoriality' played out on the ground; how it was used or perhaps abused; how Mixed Court proceedings were interpreted and acted on by Chinese economic agents and by the Chinese-language media at large.

There has recently been to my knowledge only one comprehensive English-language study of Shanghai's legal system that is informed by extensive archival fieldwork; regrettably unpublished, Tahirih Lee's 1990 PhD thesis draws impressively on a vast array of Mixed Court records preserved in the UK National Archives and, to a much less extent, on Chinese-language material. She argues that the Mixed Court 'became a means for directing the development of Shanghai according to a European model of urban growth'; that its judgements 'secured ownership of wealth and land'; that 'thousands of Chinese landlords, merchants and bankers, even the Shanghai district magistrate, used the court to settle their disputes'; and that 'confidential correspondence show that local Chinese merchants and lawyers pressed for Chinese control of the court, *but* they wished to retain its western-style procedure and its freedom to enforce local laws and customs'.[26]

The subtext of Lee's case study is whether the Mixed Court was simply an imperialistic construct designed to deepen the foreign domination of the city or whether it, in fact, ended up transmitting values that set Shanghai distinctly apart from the hinterland both materially and culturally. Much of the evidence adduced in the thesis might, however, leave readers in doubt. We are told, for example, that Mixed Court procedures and verdicts 'always tended to be pro-plaintiff'; the plaintiffs themselves were almost invariably foreign individuals, municipal utilities, and the SMP, while those being sued were almost invariably Chinese debtors or Chinese political activists.[27]

In the very few cases presented where Chinese were litigants and foreigners implicated in defence, the verdicts were exceedingly ambiguous. For example, in 1912 when Buddhist monks sued the Chinese lessee of a lot adjoining the international (formerly, 'Anglo-American') settlement and owned by their monastery for transferring land rights to the SMC without their knowledge so that the latter could build a road across, the Assessor delivered a 'long and confused' verdict that recognized the priests' claim but affirmed the SMC's right to expropriate land for roadwork with a level of compensation entirely at the latter's discretion.[28]

One would tend to associate any notion of entrenched property rights in the city with a well-developed mechanism for Sino-foreign commercial-dispute arbitration or, more generally, a local body of civil law. However, 'a blurry line' separated civil and criminal cases at the court.[29] The statistics presented by Lee suggest that between 1918 and 1926 civil disputes brought before the Mixed Court never exceeded 5% of the caseload with the bulk involving Sikhs suing Chinese for petty debts (124–126). On the rare occasion when Chinese pressed charges against another Chinese party – the Mixed Court appears to have been reluctant to intervene, or to have fallen back on 'local custom' and traditional guild punitive action. Twenty-two lawsuits by Chinese policyholders against their Chinese insurance firms are recorded, for example, but most of these were 'discontinued'.[30]

Uneven law enforcement appears as a matter of course. In 1925, for example, Edward Ezra – a successful businessman and one of the pillars of the city's 2,000-strong, elitist and Anglicised Baghdadi-Jewish community – had the SMP arrest a Chinese resident for re-selling a stash of opium, which Ezra claimed was his and not yet paid for. Ezra himself was able to dodge prosecution during the trial, although opium dealership was illegal and evidence surfaced that he had engaged in extortion.[31]

Indeed, in a later contribution to a special issue of the *Journal of Asian Studies*, Lee has portrayed the city's legal system as porous:[32]

> On the one hand, the foreign laws promised a reasonably objective and impartial standard for managing private affairs, while on the other, the existence of different [municipal] jurisdictions . . . meant that individuals and businesses could skirt the law when it did not favour them by shifting from one [concession area] to another. In Shanghai, then, one could either appeal to the law when it served one's purpose or frequently could avoid the restrictions and penalties of the law by moving back and forth among the International Settlement, the French Concession, and the Chinese administered section of the city.

If anything, the issue of justice and law enforcement is one of relativity for Chinese disputants could probably expect much less in the way of formal legal remedy in the 'Native City'. Though much less is known about legal proceedings there, W.A. Thomas's important study tells us of a 1897 case where Chinese majority shareholders in a British-registered firm sought the *daotai*'s assistance in repelling demands by the firm's British executives for additional capital contribution. This was after the Mixed Court had refused to hear their case, and after the executives' stand had received British consular endorsement. To add insult to injury, the *daotai*'s categorical response was that Sino-foreign joint ventures were not provided for under the Qing legal code, and therefore the Chinese investors were not deserving of any protection.[33]

As indicated above, native-place bonds and local custom were very important among Chinese residents of what ultimately was a city of migrants and expatriates. Bryna Goodman ably set these factors vis-à-vis the foreign presence, and its impact on the city and China beyond. Hers, in a sense, is a book that deftly charts the middle ground between China-centeredness and overstatement of foreign agency. By foregrounding a spate of confrontations between the foreign municipal authorities and a Ningbo migrant guild over the operation of a local cemetery, beginning as early as 1874, she shows how Western-style hygiene in the "model settlement" could serve as pretext for a naked land-grab, and the degree of Chinese resistance and embitterment that it aroused. Notably, Goodman also shows that, in a similar confrontation, the Mixed Court could be specifically targeted by Chinese rioters precisely because it was seen as arbitrary and impervious, as was the case in 1905.[34]

## A 'Missed Opportunity'?

Any attempt to summarize in a few sentences the academic discourse on pre-war Shanghai prior to the opening of the Municipal Archives is at risk of banalising what is an immensely erudite body of work which remains, for the most part, uncontroverted. That said, it might be fair to say that conventional wisdom until the late 1980s had cast the city as kind of 'Missed Opportunity': a bridgehead of Western civilization in the heart of autocratic China that did not accomplish its reformative mission either because it was drowned out by the sheer scale of underdevelopment in the hinterland, as Rhoads Murphey suggested; or because the Western-inspired 'gentry democracy' in Nanshi was nipped in the bud in 1914, as Mark Elvin argued in his groundbreaking PhD dissertation; or because the 'golden age' of bourgeoisie activism was cut short by the KMT rise to power in the late 1920s, as Marie-Claire Bergère showed in her now-classic study.[35]

To some extent, the 'missed opportunity' metonym is tempered by more recent quantitative work – like that carried out by Cheng, Linsun, Ma Debin and Tahirih Lee. This work paints a success story of local entrepreneurial dynamism that, because it was subsumed under extra-territoriality, could feed the city's prosperity despite the political instability in China at large. That metonym has, however, transmuted elsewhere into a debate about the legacy of the Nanjing decade (1927–1936) in Shanghai or, more strictly speaking, about the performance of the municipal government instated by the KMT after its occupation of the city in 1927.

In *Policing Shanghai*, the late Frederic Wakeman examined the

KMT record in reducing crime in Nanshi, as a litmus test for the efficiency and reach of Republican nation-building. On 7 July 1927, General Huang Fu was installed with much fanfare as the first KMT mayor amid hopes that he would undermine the rationale for extra-territoriality by making the 'Native City' even more spectacular than its neighboring foreign concessions.[36] Wakeman then shows how the mayoralty quickly changed hands from one uniformed functionary to another, as KMT practical priorities shifted from urban recon-struction to rooting out Communist cells in the city's labour movement; these changing priorities meant that the KMT did not confront Japanese expansionism head-on and, to the astonishment of most petty urbanites, closely collaborated with the SMP in crack-ing down on leftist radicals.

By 1932, the threat of radicalism had abated and General Wu Tiecheng, who was seen as less tolerant of Japan, was appointed mayor. The beginning of Wu's tenure coincided with the notorious Japanese bombing of the Zhabei district in retaliation for a popular boycott of Japanese goods. Despite the growing hostilities, Wu held on until 1937. He spoke English fluently and was on friendly terms with foreign and local financiers. With their support, he embarked on a number of infrastructure projects with a view to shifting the city's centre of gravity north of the foreign concession areas, as Sun Yat-sen himself had once envisioned. But, according to Wakeman, Wu's record on balance was one of failure. Despite lofty rhetoric his administration was not able to so much as clear peddlers off the streets, restore traffic controls, end currency speculation or signifi-cantly reduce armed robberies in Nanshi.[37]

Christian Henriot's comprehensive study of the Republican administration of Shanghai should be read in parallel to Wakeman's. Henriot skillfully unearths the gap between KMT rhetoric and praxis. For example, he points to the fact that the KMT apparatus in Shanghai had pleaded with the government in Nanjing to prohibit party members from taking up residence in the foreign concessions during the mayoral tenure of Zhang Dingfan (August 1927–March 1929). This was farcical as Zhang himself, who succeeded Huang Fu in the job, resided in the French concession along with countless other KMT dignitaries.[38]

Henriot also finds that native-place loyalties permeated the KMT in Shanghai, and that new mayoral appointments were followed by a tidal wave of new staff across all levels of the municipal adminis-tration reflecting, in essence, the province from which the mayor hailed. The Wu Tiecheng era was, for Henriot, one of symbolism despite genuine attempts to implement the Sun Yat-sen inspired Greater Shanghai Plan (*Da Shanghai jihua*). In October 1933, a new town hall was inaugurated in the Jiangwan district in the northern outskirts of Shanghai, and some municipal offices relocated there. By 1937, Jiangwan was also home to the Chinese city's library, museum and athletic stadium. However, the commercial center of gravity remained in the foreign-run south, not least because Wu was not able to see through the construction of port facilities in Wusong that were meant – according to the Plan – to supplant the foreign-run ones further down south along the Bund.[39]

On the upside, Henriot recounts Wu's success in establishing a water-treatment plant in Pudong with funding from Chinese merchants; and in rationalizing power supply in Nanshi by consolidating eight small power plants into two and tightening quality control of private utilities. But whether these are sufficient grounds from which to overturn, at least provisionally, Lloyd Eastman's powerful portrayal of the Republican era as "abortive" is moot.[40]

## A 'Babel' of Finance?

Henriot's exposition of native-place bonds within Shanghai's municipal administration ties in with phenomena that underlay the social fabric of pre-war Shanghai: ethnic networking, sub-ethnicity and their interplay with semi-colonialism. While Goodman's afore-mentioned study did much to illuminate the Chinese side of the equation, scholars have not yet fully mapped out the numerous foreign micro-communities and their share of economic and other activity. The ethnic matrix in Shanghai was convoluted because British subjects included, for example, a sizable Indian community, including Sikhs, Parsis, Ismailis and Baghdadi ('Babylonian') Jews who arrived via Mumbai; French subjects included a sizable Indochinese community; American subjects could imply Filipinos or Armenian-born émigrés; and among Japanese subjects one could find a few locally-naturalized Chinese businessmen or wealthy overseas Chinese from Southeast Asia.[41]

Just as Chinese nationality was often beset by regional loyalties, so too were foreign nationalities. The idiom of ethnicity and nationality could drum up or divert business from rivals. Nationality could also embody 'big business' in and of itself: many consulates charged hefty fees from wealthy Chinese residents in return for naturalizing them or registering their firms as foreign.

In view of the myriad languages and dialects spoken in pre-war Shanghai, as well as of its connotation of lewd adventurism, 'Babel' is therefore not an entirely inappropriate trope with which to re-visit how business was carried through in the city. For not only does it evoke the little-studied yet prominent role of Baghdadi Jews in the city's realty market but it also brings to mind the mystique with which the city was once associated: a number of Western novelists had likened Shanghai to 'Sodom', 'Nineveh' and, of course, 'Babylon'.[42]

The macro-level picture is, by comparison, fairly straightforward. We know, for example, that Chinese ratepayers, licensing fees and duties imposed on Chinese petty urbanites made up over half of SMC revenue by the 1920s. While Chinese residents accounted for over 90% of the population in the foreign concessions, it was not until 1927 that they won executive representation on the SMC board.[43] However, scholars still do not know if corporate ownership and management was similarly fragmented along ethnic lines and, if so, in what ratios. Fewer still are quantitative data on proprietary small businesses. There may perhaps be a danger that future research will overstate the 'Chineseness' of native-place bonds to the neglect of European 'particularisms', and the way in which they beset or negotiated impersonal trust in pre-war Shanghai.

In his captivating biography of one, Maurice Tinkler, an Englishman in the employ of the SMP, Robert Bickers subtly calls our attention to the truly universal nature of native-place networking as well of racial stereotyping. Tinkler, we are told, often complained to his sister about Scottish favoritism in SMP ranks. In order to lift his station in life in the face of Scottish "free-masonry", he decides to join formal Free-masonry, a society fabled for its reach within Shanghailander (i.e. white) society.[44]

Snubbed by upper-class Englishwomen, Tinkler nevertheless refrains from engaging Chinese prostitutes in order to maintain his "self respect". But this is presumably only because an influx of poor White Russian migrants had made Caucasian concubinage affordable in the 1920s. Tinkler fumes at his sister for dating a Japanese gentleman back in England but, curiously enough, does not appear to resent local Sikh policemen or Jewish shopkeepers.[45]

Sex and racial purity were not, of course, an exclusively white preoccupation. As early as 1874, Ningbo guildsmen lambasted intercourse between Cantonese prostitutes and French clients as racially defiling amid a campaign to avert the takeover of a local cemetery by the French municipal council.[46] But despite the jeopardy of excommunication, a few Sino-foreign couples did defiantly wed and jointly climbed up the slippery social ladder of Shanghai: such were the marriage of the enigmatic Baghdadi-Jewish realty mogul Silas Hardoon, and a devoutly Buddhist waif;[47] Inspector E.W. Everson, the SMP officer who ordered fire at Chinese strikers, thereby unleashing the May Thirtieth Incident (1925) – the most serious Sino-Foreign confrontation in the city during the pre-war era – was ironically one of few Britons married to Chinese.[48]

In the private as well as mercantile realms, there were myriad ineffable Sino-foreign 'cross-border' liaisons that underlay everyday life beneath the veneer of rigid racial and class distinction, but about which we still know relatively little. At least one Mixed Court record suggests as much: it delineates a love affair between Lika, a Sikh, and his married Chinese neighbor Wang Ni. The affair evolves into a court case since Lika is eventually stabbed to death by Wang's cuckolded husband, whom the foreign municipal authorities want for manslaughter but Chinese customary law holds innocent on account of the adultery committed by the deceased.[49]

The contours of the Sino-Foreign encounter at the 'big end of town' are clearer thanks to pioneering work by Wang Jingyu, Hao Yen-p'ing, Andrea McElderry, Motono Eiichi, and Nishimura Shizuya.[50] When read together, their work seems to allude that Chinese capital funded much, if not most, of the foreign-run joint-stock company capitalization in the pre-war era. The British Joint Stock Companies Act laid the foundations of modern company law only in 1856, and it is perhaps not sufficiently recognized that this milestone in world economic history was immediately transplanted by British entrepreneurs based in East Asia. But in applying the principles of joint-stock incorporation there had always been a key difference between Hong Kong and Shanghai that needs to be thoroughly examined. While the Crown Colony government, under pressure from its mercantile community, localized the new company law principles through its 1865 Companies Ordinance – Whitehall was reluctant to fully apply the mechanics of joint-stock enterprise to Shanghai's semi-colonial setting.[51]

Without comprehensive consular recognition, and even though Chinese company law was virtually non-existent before 1904, foreign and domestic joint-stock company prospectuses appeared in Shanghai as early as the 1870s, and stock trading flourished. It was only in 1907 that firms could register in the British consulate as a cheaper substitute to maintaining an office in Hong Kong. The British Consular Supreme Court in the international concession assumed full responsibility for regulating joint-stock companies only through a 1915 Order-in-Council, which provided that any company applying for registration as British in Shanghai must maintain a majority of British directors, and that its chief manager must be a British subject.[52]

What has perhaps not been sufficiently explained is how, despite the earlier and more robust foundation of company law in Hong Kong, the foreign-run bourse in Shanghai eventually outshone that of the Crown Colony in the pre-war era. This is an important question not least because the pre-war state of play is starkly different to how the Shanghai bourse has fared vis-à-vis Hong Kong's since 1991. Foreign-run company shares were traded in Shanghai as early as 1866 and eagerly taken up by Chinese investors who later shunned Chinese joint-stock ventures. How, despite its seemingly porous legal system, was foreign-run Shanghai able to prosper and attract so much Chinese capital?[53]

Alongside bank loans and government investment, the volume and tradability of equity was often a critical determinant of industrialization in early-modern economies. Chinese stock and commodity exchanges had organically evolved in Shanghai by the early1880s, but remained small, diffuse and largely dormant thereafter. What impinged most on equity trade was frequent Court interference in the managerial affairs of listed companies. This interference deterred potential investors and brought China's primary indigenous stock exchange to a virtual standstill by mid-1880s. Subsequent attempts to revive equity markets were made in the 1920s, but these were similarly beset by government inability to reassure investors or enshrine property rights.[54]

## The 21st Century

Since 1991, Shanghai has transformed itself from a city strongly associated in Mao's era (1949–1976) with heavy industry, central planning and ideological zealotry to arguably the PRC's most important finance and R&D hub. This transformation was accomplished through "fiscal federalism" which incentivized municipal authorities to court private investment, and allowed them to retain a higher share of local revenue in return. The transformation was also accomplished through central-government prioritizing of Shanghai over other urban centers. Emphasis on Shanghai-led development peaked during Jiang Zemin's presidency (1993–2003), and is still seen today as his loyalists' (*Shanghai bang*) cause. The late Huang Ju, an erstwhile mayor and Jiang loyalist, once declared: 'Shanghai of the future must be a metropolis equal to New York or London.'[55]

If scholars are to provide a persuasive account of Shanghai's contribution to China in the *longue durée*, then it is crucial to pinpoint the similarities as well as differences between the pre-war era, the Mao era and the current reform setting. Rudolf Wagner suggested, for example, that the Special Economic Zones, which inform the current reform thrust, were an attempt to resurrect the treaty-port development path while neutering the democratic potential which it had once spawned.[56] Yet the question today, as in the pre-war era, can be amplified: has Shanghai ever had a truly free-wheeling spirit, or was it simply a case of lawlessness glorified and institutions misconstrued?

Another important question which transcends rigid epochal boundaries is whether Shanghai's economic success has been due to foreign or Chinese agency. Does Shanghai today rise economically above other cities despite or because of Chinese government intervention? For the debate among economists over the PRC's performance still centers around the question of whether growth is mainly sustained by foreign investment in offshore assembly lines, or by Chinese rural and private-sector vibrancy.[57]

Even the current problematic of Shanghai's stock exchange inevitably invokes the pre-war setting. Though there is no longer a competing foreign-run bourse operating along side the one regulated by the Chinese government, there have re-emerged vexed issues concerning the bureaucratic manipulation of board decisions, poor accounting transparency and private investors' rights. Nonetheless, within the global financial system Hong Kong's equity market is now – in contrast to the pre-war state of play – more vital to foreign and Chinese firms than Shanghai's, and its performance much more closely correlated with PRC economic growth figures.[58]

The disparity between Shanghai and rural China is every bit as staggering today as it was in the pre-war era, if not worse. It is thrown into relief when compared with other emerging economies:

official statistics put Shanghai's per capita GDP in 2003 at US$ 4,516 – nearly five times the All-China average. That year, per capita GDP in Mumbai (US$ 931), while much lower than in Shanghai, was only twice the Indian average. São Paulo's GDP (US$ 4,023), by comparison, was only 1.38 higher than the Brazilian average.[59]

Whether or not the Shanghai–hinterland divide will diminish over time, it seems safe to speculate that the city's cosmopolitan heritage will loom larger as China rapidly re-integrates with the international community to assume a leading role.[60] The marketing potency of "memory-lane" is already evidenced in massive housing redevelopment projects and theme shopping centres, such as Xintiandi, in what was once the French concession. Xintiandi ingeniously harps on the plebeian hustle and bustle but its residents today are much wealthier than the concession's *lilong* petty urbanites once were. There may be, in that sense, a growing appetite for a certain 'Old Shanghai' chic and mystique on the part of China's new rich. It is, at the same time, the job of historians to de-mystify that very 'Old Shanghai' with quotidian facts, rudimentary statistics and archival evidence.

## Notes

1 Wasserstrom (2009); Menzel (2006).
2 Wu and Ma (2003).
3 See e.g. Du (2002).
4 Lu (1998); Xiong and Zhou (2004)
5 See in particular Cheng (2003). For the more widely accepted view of Shanghai financiers as submitting to KMT corporatism during the Nanjing decade (1927–1937), see in particular, Bergère (1986); Bergère (2002); Coble (1980); Fewsmith (1985); Ji (2002).
6 See in particular Tang (1989). See also, for example, Liu (1985); and Xiong (1999). Recent valuable PRC compilations include Tang (1989); Zhou and Tang (1999); *Reprints of the Minutes of the SMC Executive Committee* (2001) as well as material surveyed in periodicals like *Dang'an yu shixue* [Archives and Historical Studies] and *Shanghai dang'an* [Shanghai Archives].
7 See Fairbank (1969); Lu (1999); Johnson, (1995).
8 Cohen (1984); Chakrabarty (2000).
9 Lu (1999), *passim*.
10 Johnson (1995); MacPherson (1996).
11 Some of Lu's earlier work (e.g. 1992) seems more attuned to the limits of city development before the arrival of the British. For a discussion

of how Western-style municipal services, medicine and hygienic consciousness filtered via Shanghai to other treaty-ports and China beyond, see MacPherson (1987) and Rogaski (2004).

12 Lee (2001), pp. 23–42, 82–119; Pan (2008), *passim*.

13 Lu (1999), p. 21. For critique of Johnson's (1995) position, see Bickers (1997).

14 American scholarly work informed by the notion of a burgeoning 'public sphere' along Habermasian lines in pre-war China include Rowe (1984); Rankin (1986); and Strand (1989). For recent Chinese scholars' perspectives on this issue, see, for example, Hong (2007) and Wang (2007).

15 See Wakeman (1993). For a fairly similar argument focusing on Republican-era corporatism, see Bergère (1997). For a middle-ground, primary-source based assessment of whether a European-style 'civil society', 'public sphere' or transparent democratic processes existed in Chinese Shanghai circa 1918, see Goodman's excellent recent study (2000a). Notably, Goodman finds a 'language of elections', 'gesture(s) toward democratization' yet 'lax voting procedures' (55–56, 58) by elites governing native-place guilds rather than actual elections for office. The guilds did eventually embrace some Western forms of representative political engagement but these were 'far from transparent' (85).

16 Wagner (1995).

17 For Wager's critique of Reed (2004), see: http://mclc.osu.edu/rc/pubs/reviews/wagner.htm [Accessed 9 November 2013].

18 Ye (2004); Wang, (2007); Wagner (1999). On the staidness of *Shenbao* 申報 compared to other Chinese-language newspapers, see, for example, Goodman (1995), pp.142–143 (in relation to *Huibao* 匯報 invectives during the famous Yang Yuelou   marriage scandal); Judge (1996), p. 40 (in relation to the reformist *Shibao*   ); notably, *Shenbao* and *Hubao* 滬報 – though both initially British-owned – did not enjoy British extra-territorial immunity. See, for example, Wagner (1999); Goodman (2000b); Mittler (2004); and Meng (2006).

19 See Clifford (1991); Bickers (1999). Cf. Wood (1998); Bickers and Wasserstrom (1995); Xu (2001), pp. 175–177.

20 MacPherson (1996), p. 499.

21 For a discussion on how Shanghai took over the other treaty-ports, see Horesh (2009).

22 Zhou (2004).

23 Xu (2001), pp. 181–183.

24 Ma (2004).

25 Ma (2008) On pre-war Shanghai's consumer culture, see also Cochran (1999); Laing (2004); Yeh (2007). On the labor movement, see Chesneaux (1962); Rigby (1980); Honig (1986); Roux (1993); and

Perry (1993). On organized crime, see Wakeman (1995); and Martin (1996).

26 See Lee (1990). For a similar argument, see Stephens (1992). For a recent Chinese study of the Mixed Court, see Yang (2006).

27 Lee (1990), pp. 9, 13, 125.

28 Lee (1990), pp. 34–44.

29 Lee (1990), p. 183.

30 Lee (1990), pp. 58–59, 143, 306–309. For recent Chinese studies of the city's pre-war Jewish community as a whole, see Xu (2007); and Wang (2008).

31 Lee (1990), pp. 184–185.

32 Lee (1995), p. 5.

33 Thomas (2001), pp. 88–89. The *daotai* does, however, seem to have adjudicated purely Chinese shareholder disputes after the promulgation of imperial company law in 1904. In 1907, the newly formed Chinese Shanghai General Chamber of Commerce (*Shanghai zong shanghui*) called for more comprehensive legal reform, citing a case where the British Privy Council ruled in favour of Chinese clients of the British-run Chartered Bank who were owed money by the bank's comprador. See Faure (2006), pp. 63–64.

34 Goodman (1995), pp. 158–175, 187–195.

35 Elvin's (1967) dissertation was ground-breaking by virtue of its meticulous analysis of British diplomatic archival material and, not least, due to the fact that it presaged the academic debate on the existence of a Habermasian 'civil society' in Shanghai well before the very same concept was popularized in the field of Chinese Studies. See also Murphey (1974); Bergère (1986). For a more recent and somewhat more qualified iteration of Bergère's approach, see Xu (2001), pp. 105–106.

36 Wakeman (1995), pp. 44–45.

37 Wakeman (1995), p. 291.

38 Henriot (1993), pp. 43, 75–76, 109–110.

39 Henriot (1993), pp. 181–183.

40 Henriot (1993), pp. 173–175, 234–235; Eastman (1974).

41 For recent studies of the Japanese community in pre-war Shanghai, see Fogel (2000); Chen (2007); and Takatsuna, (2009).

42 Miller (1994), pp. 239–345. For a recent Chinese study of the city's pre-war foreign business community, see Wang (2007).

43 Thomas (2001), p. 60.

44 Bickers (2003), pp. 135–137. On the racial matrix in Shanghai and its interplay with semi-colonialism in Asia, see Bickers and Henriot (2000).

45 Bickers (2003). On anti-Semitism in pre-war Shanghai, see also Finnane (1999) and Ristaino (2001), pp. 48–49.

46 Goodman (1995), pp. 169–170. On racist stereotyping of Europeans, see also Wasserstrom (1998).
47 On Hardoon, see the pioneering studies of Chiara (1997) and Meyer (2003).
48 On Everson, see Bickers (1999), p. 74.
49 Lee (1990), pp. 23–29. For a discussion of Sino-Foreign 'Border-Crossers' in pre-war Shanghai and their importance, see Wasserstrom (2008). For brief coverage of the commoditised physical contact between Chinese and expatriates in pre-war Shanghai, see, for example, Henriot's magisterial study (2001), pp. 99–101, 108, 158, and Hershatter's equally authoritative book (1997), pp. 50–53).
50 Wang (1965); Hao (1970); McElderry (1976); Motono (2000); Nishimura (2005).
51 Thomas (2001), p. 29. On the belated evolution of Chinese company law, see Kirby (1995).
52 Thomas (2001), pp. 31–32.
53 For a tentative preliminary overview of the Shanghai bourse today and before World War II, see for example, Chen (2006).
54 Hong (1989); McElderry (2001).
55 Wu (2007), p. 115; Wu (2007), p. 211.
56 Wagner (1995), pp. 442–443. For important work that aims to deal with Shanghai in the *longue durée*, see for example, Howe (1981); Yeung (1996); and Gamble (2003).
57 On this debate, see Qian (2002) and Huang (2008).
58 Chen (2006), pp. 39–40.
59 Raiser and Volkmann (2007), p. 342.
60 He (2007), pp. 179–181. On Shanghai's putative new cosmopolitanism, see also Farrer (2008).

# 3

# The Early Rise of a Treaty-Port,
# 1840s–1860s

In his path-breaking volume *Remaking the Chinese City*, Professor Joseph Esherick famously complained that Western historiography of 20th-century China had been marred by a 'singular focus on Shanghai'.[1] In other words, while Shanghai's pre-war history (1842–1937) was already 'quite well understood' thanks to an inordinately large number of studies, other Chinese urban centres have merely invited scant attention. A number of Western scholars have since shifted their gaze elsewhere in search of other Chinese articulations of modernity – most notably Ruth Rogaski and Frank Dikötter.[2]

Yet a thorough examination of the history of other Chinese cities – as timely as it may be – cannot replace a continual robust engagement with Shanghai. This is not least because the vast array of materials available at the Shanghai Municipal Archives (SMA) and Zikawei Library have been systematically catalogued only since the late 2000s. They are indispensable to understanding the city's rise to prominence and its preponderant position within China's economic modernization process. While some Chinese and Western scholars have already addressed themselves to these newly-available materials,[3] the latter remains relatively under-studied.

Mainly drawing on rare early editions of the *North-China Herald* (NCH) held at the Zikawei Library, this chapter will highlight one aspect of Shanghai's early treaty-port development; it will reprise the conventional wisdom positing that, because of its perceived advantageous location, Shanghai had been almost deterministically poised to become China's gateway to the outside world following the First Opium War (1839–1842). Instead, it will argue that location was significant but not *sufficient* of itself in delivering Shanghai's economic take-off.

The following passages admittedly draw much less on the vast SMA repository than on *Herald* accounts. This is because the documentary material in SMA, while invaluable to our understanding of Shanghai's development after 1870, contains relatively little on the formative era under review here (1840s–1860s). Shanghai Municipal Council (SMC) documents from that era are not likely to be found in great quantity elsewhere either, since they had been primarily stored in the British Consulate compound, which was gutted by fire on 23 December 1870.[4]

Geography looms large in much of the classic Western scholarship on pre-war Shanghai. Most notably, Rhoads Murphey's influential work (1953) all but entrenched the notion that 'the physical advantages of the city's location' was the most important factor in its take-off as a treaty-port. Though tempered by more recent multi-faceted studies, the emphasis on geographical location is still quite pervasive in the pertinent literature. Indeed, Shanghai's 'propitious location', its appeal as a 'natural pivot point for trade', or as '*grand port côtier*' are discussed at considerable length in some of the best newly-published work on the city's history.[5]

Drawing on colonial records preserved in the UK National Archives, Linda Johnson's monograph (1995) is perhaps one of the most detailed Western studies of Shanghai between the 1840s and 1860s. Interestingly enough, at least half of her book is dedicated to an exposition of Shanghai as an important Chinese urban centre *prior* to the arrival of British settlers (CE 1074–1840, Chapters 1–6). The exposition is, in that sense, emphatically China-centred, a theoretical approach first accredited to Paul Cohen;[6] it runs counter to the old colonial myth suggesting that Shanghai had been an inconsequential 'fishing village' before Europeans landfall turned it into a 'model settlement'.[7]

Notably, Johnson attributes much of the city's dynamism after 1840 to the " . . . development of a public sphere serving public interests, independent of both British and Chinese governments", in both the British-run and Chinese-run precincts. Put baldly, her argument is that the city's spectacular growth owes much to Chinese agency both before and after 1842, not just to European municipal administration and maritime trade.[8]

As in Johnson's work, this chapter will highlight Chinese settlement in the city's foreign concessions in the mid-1850s as a critical factor in their subsequent prosperity. Yet the analysis offered here is comparative; it is underpinned by a re-assessment of the significance of geographical location as compared with other possible factors ranging from the fundamental to the incidental. In that sense, the thematic question posed at the background of this study is the inverse of the one posed by Johnson: if Shanghai's physical location had been so compelling, why was it not among China's ten biggest cities on the eve of European settlement? Indeed, the question almost begs itself in view of authoritative geo-historical surveys of the area.[9]

To be sure, given its limited temporal scope, this chapter cannot purport to 're-write history' or trivialize the great significance of Shanghai's location. It will nonetheless underscore that Shanghai's location posed just as many difficulties for the first European settlers, and that scepticism about the future prospects of the city was initially rife for that reason. How these difficulties were subsequently overcome is a story of clearly institutional, technological and fiscal dimensions – it is one that remains under-studied. These dimensions cannot be fully treated here. But, at the very least, the following passages might draw greater attention to additional factors that might help explain Shanghai's growth after 1842.

## Location or Rebellion and Fiscal Breakthrough?

The reasons why the British chose Shanghai as their primary military and commercial node in China, and negotiated for its territorial concession as part of the Nanjing Treaty (1842), are complex. The East India Company's (EIC) explorer Hugh Hamilton Lindsay, and inveterate missionaries Karl Gützlaff and W.H. Medhurst's respective travelogues, are often cited as the most important factor in bringing Shanghai's virtues to British consciousness in the 1830s, namely, on the eve of China's opening up to foreign trade after centuries in which this trade had been confined to Canton.[10] Notable too was the influence Dr William Jardine – veteran China Hand, surgeon turned opium trader, Shanghai aficionado, and later Member of Parliament – exerted over the British foreign secretary, Lord Palmerston, in the lead-up to the first Opium War.[11]

Canton [Guangzhou] had become an anathema for the British by then because it was commonly associated with monopolistic practices by both Chinese merchant guilds (the Hongs) and the EIC, as well as with hostile Imperial commissioners (the Hoppos) and xenophobic mobs. The British had, of course, aimed at opening up other ports further north in order to sustain their grip on global commodity trade, and realize the potential of opium imports in China's hinterland markets.[12]

The Nanjing Treaty of 1842, which ended the first Opium War, eventually provided for the opening of four such additional ports north of Canton: Xiamen [Amoy], Fuzhou, Ningbo and Shanghai. The few British settlers who arrived at these ports the following year were happy to discover that locals showed little of the ' . . . turbulent spirit so conspicuously manifested at Canton'; the northernmost port of the four, Shanghai, was seen as bearing great potential for trade by some, but ' . . . few at the time foresaw the great position it was ultimately to reach'.[13]

In the first few years since its opening, both domestic and international trade flows via Shanghai were sluggish, and there was little sign of a turnaround in sight. The British, who were keen to uncork the Canton trade confinement, were understandably frustrated. On July 1844, for example, the first British Consul posted to the city, Captain George Balfour, demanded that the highest-ranking Qing official in the region, Taotai Gong Mujiu, explain why there had not been progress in domestic trade. Gong reported that overland tea consignments en route to Shanghai had been diverted back to Canton in Jiangxi. Gong then assured Balfour that he intervened with the Jiangxi sub-prefects to allow north-bound traffic.[14] As late as 1853, Rutherford Alcock, the proactive British Consul who succeeded Balfour, and is often credited with turning around Shanghai's lot, still described it as an 'isolated sea-port on the coast of a vast Empire'.[15]

Ironically, a good deal of scepticism about the city's future was expressed precisely because of its location not far from the mouth of the Huangpu River at Wusong [Woosung]. This was the cause of constant navigational problems in the first few decades after European settlement because of downstream silting. Between the 1840s and until the British-run municipality amassed enough fiscal revenue to launch extensive dredging in the 1880s, the Wusong sandbar had become synonymous with maritime hardship. The British Parliamentary *Hansard* suggests that even as late as 1874 Shanghai's small foreign community (predominantly merchants and missionaries – British, French, American – and a few Parsis and Baghdadi Jews) was hopeful that the Chinese government would fund the dredging of this sandbar out of its own pocket.

A well-informed short history of the city, published in 1928, cast the dredging of the Bar in the 1880s as a veritable milestone in the city's development:[16]

> The accessibility of the harbour in Shanghai was rendered difficult by the shallow water over the outer and inner Woosung Bars. These are formed by the tidal Whang-poo [Huangpu] River emptying itself into the tidal estuary of the Yangtze River. The low water depth of the river bar varied in different months of the year from 6 feet to 13 feet 6 inches and was in the midst of a crossing that cut diagonally from one bank to the other of the Whang-poo River . . . .
>
> In 1863 when Robert Hart, Inspector-General of Customs, was in Shanghai, a deputation, representing the leading shipping firms, put before him the importance of conserving the Whangpoo and of dredging the Woosung Bar, so as to allow the entrance of the larger ships then being dispatched to China. He agreed to lay the matter before The Chinese Government . . . .
>
> To all requests the answer of the Chinese Government was 'No,' and the Chinese Ministers maintained an attitude 'even more obstructive than the obstruction of the Bar.' It is well to remember that in the early days, the Chinese sometimes referred to the bar as a heaven-sent barrier intended to prevent war vessels of heavy draught and ironclads from entering the harbour.

Sir Robert Hart, alongside Alcock, is conventionally credited with anchoring Shanghai as Britain's primary bastion in China. Yet the very same Hart, who presided over the Chinese Imperial Maritime Customs Service (IMCS), had predicted in the early 1860s that steam technology and the opening of the Suez Canal would end up diverting trade from Shanghai even if the Bar was properly dredged:[17]

> [I]n 20 years time Chinkiang [Jinjiang, Fujian] will have taken the place of Shanghai as a semi-terminus and trans-shipment port . . .Thus looked at, as it affects and is affected by natural and artificial agencies now at work at the mouth of the Yangtze, the question of the Woosung Bar is seen to mean that dredging there may possibly be nothing more than a means of making the last days of Shanghai a little more comfortable than they would otherwise be; it will not prolong or avert the commercial death of the place, but it will make a show of vitality during its declining years more possible.

To understand how the British-run SMC was eventually able to amass enough resources to transform the city's physical setting; to remove such geographical obstructions and to secure its future growth as a port – scholars must first turn their mind to 1853. For, as indicated above, trade emanating from Shanghai had been fairly sluggish hitherto.

Then, happenstance intervened: an obscure band of misfits, the Small Sword Society (*xiaodao hui*), rebelled against the local Qing authorities in Shanghai's 'Native City', driving the Taotai's Imperial forces out.[18] The disruption to law and order was such that as many as 22,000 refugees escaped the walled, old city of Shanghai to seek refuge in the areas strung along the Yang-king-pang [*Yangjingbang*] Canal, which demarcated the border between British and French settlements within the concession area.

J.D. Clark's well-informed *Short History of Shanghai* is one of countless pre-war sources suggesting that this was a crucial turn-around in the city's early treaty-port history.[19] The unchecked wave of refugees ended, in effect, an era in which only Europeans and the indigenous rural population sparsely scattered along the Bund could reside in the concession area (1843–1852). From then on, the SMC could extract exorbitant fees from wealthy Chinese refugees for the smallest of municipal services. Similarly, European lessees of concessionary land – foreign land-ownership *per se* was never recognized by the Qing – could provide makeshift accommodation for the wealthier amongst the refugees at inflated prices.

The Qing Imperial forces were able to recover the 'Native City' from Small Sword rebels and restore order south of the *Yangjingbang* by early 1855. Yet an even larger exodus of refugees converged on Shanghai from all over the Lower Yangtze Delta (Jiangnan) seven years later, as the broader Taiping Rebellion swept through the region in 1862. This second exodus consisted of as many as 110,000 refugees, with many carrying along their lifetime savings in silver bullion, then China's primary mercantile means of payment. By 1862, word of the foreigners' determination to protect the concession area from both Qing and Rebel encroachment – as first demonstrated during the Small Sword upheaval – had spread far and wide; it rightly persuaded many that the concessions were the safest place to flee to.[20]

## Other Factors: Land Grab, Customs Takeover, Consular Proactivity

Once Qing forces had quashed the Small Sword rebellion in January 1855, Alcock feigned cooperation with Taotai orders that Chinese refugees north of the *Yangjingbang* return to the 'Native City'. Yet, the refugees had proven such a bonanza to the municipal authorities that Alcock, the American Consul, Robert C. Murphy, and the French Consul B. Edan, ratified a new set of Land Regulations in July 1854, which ran counter to the Taotai's orders, and were never subsequently ratified by him.

The old Land Regulations were derived from the Treaty of the Bogue (1843), which in turn supplemented the Nanjing Treaty. They provided for foreigners' rights to lease land along the Bund and north of the 'Native City', and to maintain judicial autonomy therein, but precluded Chinese residency in these foreign concessions.

By contrast, the new Regulations (1854) meant in effect that all foreign lessees of land in the concession area could eventually acquire title-deeds and, equally important, that Chinese newcomers could rent accommodation anywhere within the concession areas. Before long, Chinese residents far outnumbered foreigners, and the era of segregation between Europeans and Chinese was consigned to a footnote in the city's annals.[21]

The new Land Regulations formalized a *fait accompli*: between 1845 and 1853 many agile foreign lessees of concessionary land scrambled to buy out the original Chinese landowners in anticipation of an imminent rise in demand for housing. It seems most paid very little to the original landowners. So much so that on 14 January 1854, shortly before the new Regulations come into effect, Alcock published the following Notification in the *NCH*:[22]

Many applications for allotments within the limits of the land originally set apart for the residence of British subjects by the local authorities have been recently made. In some cases, land appears to have been taken over without either previous notice or reference to this office – a proceeding only calculated to give rise to dissensions and litigations. Her-Majesty's Consul desires under these circumstances to warn the community of the necessity for great caution in any dealings for land in the present unsettled state of affairs at the port . . . To the purchase of land from Chinese at this time, there are two very serious objections. The one is the impossibility of obtaining a legal title . . . The other is the virtual abeyance of the [old] Land Regulations now under the consideration of the higher Authorities . . . The sudden demand for house accommodation and more land, occasioned by the large influx of Chinese seeking shelter and security in the Foreign settlement . . . has indeed proved both the necessity and the difficulty of adhering to this course of action . . . The old regulations still in existence prohibit to Chinese and Foreigners alike the building or renting of houses within the limits for the Native population. In the draft of the new [Land regulations] all restriction in this particular has been omitted.

Notably, the Qing loss of land rights within the concession area in the mid-1850s was compounded by the loss of tariff autonomy. Until the Small Sword Rebellion, the Chinese Customhouse in the 'Native City' had been responsible for collecting duties from junks and steamers entering city bounds. This upset many British merchants, who saw the Chinese Customhouse as corrupt. However, the Customhouse was deserted when the Small Sword rebels moved in, and no duties were collected for almost two years afterwards, effectively turning Shanghai into a free port and a haven for smugglers.

Though Alcock let British vessels evade duties during that period, he was becoming increasingly concerned that unbridled trade would advantage other European nations. Therefore, once order had been restored in the 'Native City', he astutely wrested control over duty collection from foreign vessels by offering the Taotai a share of the revenue, and the allurement of unburdening the local Qing bureaucracy from dealing with 'barbarian' crewmen.[23]

As indicated above, the British bypass of Chinese tariff autonomy, its allotment of land rights within the concession area, as well as the influx of rent-paying refugees all had sweeping fiscal implications. To better understand these, we must examine Shanghai's finances before the Small Sword Rebellion, i.e. during the era of effective segregation between foreigners and Chinese.

A rare hand-written report pertaining to the SMC, now stored at SMA, poignantly bears out the Council's difficulties in raising taxes from the small foreign community with which to fund capital works during the era of segregation. This 'Report of the Committee of the Shanghae Roads and Jetties for the Year Ending May 18th 1852' [sic] states:[24]

The Committee regrets having to report parties who have refused to pay Jetty Tax, and one party [who refused to pay] the Road Assessment . . . the late rain enables the Committee to point forcibly to the Meeting the injury done to the roads by the present system of carrying mud from the River to the back lots of the Settlement. The Committee are at a loss to suggest a remedy, but they feel convinced that so long as the present careless system continues, it will be utterly impossible to preserve the roads in a proper state, more especially the Bund where the mud is first landed.

By 1856, thousands of makeshift houses had been made for refugees along the *Yangjingbang*. The *Herald* reports suggest that most of these were built by European realty speculators like Gilman Bowman & Co.[25] A year before, the Taotai demanded that these 'hovels' be pulled down because they hindered navigation on the Canal, thereby obstructing Qing supply lines to the forces besieging the rebels in the walled city. Alcock seems to have used the Taotai's demands as a pretext to pressure Chinese owners of land adjacent to the Canal to share the rent collected from refugee tenants with British lessees of the same land.[26]

Increasing municipal land-tax revenue and tariff-derived funds meant that law and order, roads and port facilities could be improved in order to stimulate trade and secure Shanghai's future as the leading British bastion in China proper. In the short-term, law and order were most important because they entrenched Shanghai's comparative advantage as an island of stability in a vast empire with an atrophying central government that was buffeted by rebellions and foreign encroachment.

The SMC's report for 1855 suggests that land-tax receipts from Chinese residents (3,179 silver dollars) had exceeded by then foreign receipts ($2,249). The great bulk of municipal revenue ($11,728) was derived from wharfage fees – but here the distinction between Chinese junks and ocean-going western vessels is impossible to pare down. Notably, of a total expenditure of $20,520, over half was spent on police procurement and wages, and only $7,000 on new roads and jetties. Overall the SMC could conclude its performance that year on an upbeat note:[27]

The Council are happy to report that a material change for the better has taken place [in the Settlement] . . . In addition to the improvement arising from increased jetty accommodation; more extended and better made thoroughfares, and from a more complete system of drains, the streets have been lighted and kept almost entirely free from beggars, and the nuisances of various kinds by which, formerly, foreigners were so seriously inconvenienced. The Chinese buildings on the Yang-king-pang have been removed . . . [and the area] covered with native hovels, is now in the occupation of foreigners, while a period seems to have been put to the erection of buildings for the accommodation of Chinese in other quarters, and it is probable that ere long, a portion of the tenements which were so hastily constructed during the siege of the city will be abandoned by their present occupants: a step which cannot fail to contribute materially to the cleanliness and salubrity of the place . . .

Chinese studies often portray a 'violent and crafty usurpation' (*haoduo qiaoqu*) of rights from Chinese landowners in the foreign concession as part of a British imperialist grand design.[28] It is nevertheless important to note that the end of segregation between Europeans and Chinese was not welcomed by *all* Europeans in the settlement. Some members of the small European community in Shanghai, who were less associated with mercantile and realty interests, expressed grave concerns about the influx of refugees. They feared that a Chinese majority in the settlement would impinge on its flimsy infrastructure and compromise hygiene and etiquette standards.

One anonymous letter that is representative of this vein was published in the *NCH* in May 1856:[29]

The admission of Chinese residents into our settlement, although attended with pecuniary advantages to many, is in other respects and annoyance . . . [due to the] imperfect drainage of native houses (not that our own are by any means perfect) and the system of allowing all drains to run on to the roads or ditches on the road side . . .

However, these were merely minority voices in the larger sweep of events.

## The Situation in Other Ports

The previous section highlighted 1853 as a turning point in Shanghai's development trajectory. In order to understand 1853 in context, one must take account of what happened in other parts of China at the same time, particularly developments in the four other ports opened to trade following the Nanjing Treaty.

Recent work by Professor Xiong Yuezhi and other Chinese scholars draws out three important factors attending Shanghai's rise.[30] First, the wealthy Jiangnan gentry began gravitating toward Shanghai after the Small Sword Rebellion. They viewed Shanghai as a haven of stability that was largely free of Qing bureaucratic exactions common in more established urban centers like Suzhou. Second, Shanghai's large Chinese mercantile population had incorporated many migrants from various parts of China long before Europeans arrived. At the grass-roots, it was a very heterogenic society, and therefore much less suspicious of foreigners. Third, Late Qing monarchs relinquished grand public works, to the extent that the Great Canal (*da yunhe*) – once China's arterial waterway – progressively fell into disrepair. This occasioned a shift of domestic trade toward the coastline, benefiting hitherto marginal county-level towns like Shanghai.

While the Small Sword and Taiping effect on Jiangnan's gentry has been discussed at length above, the ways in which late-Imperial inertia precipitated a shift in domestic trade routes await more detailed research. For now, the shift lacks clear-cut documentary support in either PRC or Western studies. On the other hand, there is plenty of evidence to bear out the second factor, namely, the accommodating nature of Shanghai's migrant society.

In the preamble to his wonderfully animated portrayal of plebeian life in Shanghai, Professor Lu Hanchao has pointed to a number of contemporaneous testimonials to that effect. He thus concluded: "Although the rise of modern Shanghai must be explained from a multi-faceted analysis – including the favourable geographical location of the city, sitting as it does in the middle of the nation's lengthy coastline facing the Pacific to the east and the Yangtze Valley to the west – the 'soft' nature of the Shanghainese no doubt played an important role."[31]

Evidence can be easily found elsewhere too. In 1908, for example, veteran China-hand, Arnold Wright, observed:[32]

The successful and entirely harmonious establishment of the [Shanghai European] settlement was . . . in a considerable measure due to the cordial relationship which existed between the British and the Chinese authorities [there] . . . The native population also were very friendly . . . Moreover, the inhabitants were naturally of a more peaceful type than the turbulent Cantonese with whom the foreign element had formerly mainly had to deal.

However, Wright was also quick to note that, initially:[33]

. . . [the] dull and apathetic character of the natives of the place disqualified them from the bustle and energy inseparable from European commerce. At the end of the first year of its history as an open port [1843] Shanghai counted only 23 foreign residents . . . only 44 foreign vessels had arrived during the same period.

The comparatively low degree of xenophobia in Shanghai, insofar as it constituted an advantage over other ports, should not be overstated. Ningbo was another one of the five ports opened after the first Opium War. In 1857, an *NCH* dispatch from Ningbo exclaimed that " . . . at no one of the five ports are the natives more friendly than [here]".[34]

Similarly, there was much to recommend Fuzhou as an alternative port to either Canton or Shanghai. Fuzhou loomed larger in important mid-1830s accounts: the EIC's China Director, Sir James Urmston, who analysed the future prospects of Britain's trade there, underscored 'Foo-chow-fu' as an ideal port because of its proximity to the tea growing areas of Fujian province, while eliding any mention of Shanghai altogether.

When surveying the Lower Yangtze, Urmston, like many of his contemporaries, was much more engrossed in the adjacent island of Zhoushan [Chusan]. The latter had a convenient deep-water port, where the EIC had ephemerally traded in the mid-18th century. Urmston similarly commended the commercial potential of Ningbo, a 'large and populous city of the first class'.[35] Britain, it should be remembered, occupied Zhoushan during the first Opium war precisely because many thought it would prove an ideal location for trade; it was reluctantly traded off for another island, Hong Kong, as part of the Nanjing Treaty. Either way, memories of Lindsay's effusive 1834 account of Shanghai carried the day with the British naval force eventually deciding to penetrate further inland and storm the 'Native City' in 1842.[36]

As the first European settlers soon realized, the Shanghainese were less versed in foreign trade than their Southern compatriots. A *Herald* editorial from 1854 lamented the 'prejudices' of Shanghai 'natives', who insisted that foreign merchants pay for Chinese commodities in full-bodied and increasingly scarce Spanish-American (Carolus) silver dollars. By contrast, in Fuzhou, often-adulterated Mexican dollars, which European merchants could obtain more easily, were accepted by the Chinese 'with equal felicity'. This meant Chinese tea was made 25% more expensive for Europeans to purchase in Shanghai than in Fuzhou.[37]

The possibility of Fuzhou eventually overtaking Shanghai as Britain's gateway to China persisted even later that decade. In 1856, for example, a Shanghai merchant anonymously complained to the *Herald* that maritime trade in Fuzhou was not regulated by the local Chinese authorities, whereas in Shanghai duties were being strictly enforced by the newly-established British-run IMCS. This meant that tea consignments were being diverted from Shanghai to Fuzhou, whence they could be exported overseas. Summing up the implications of this loophole, the merchant soliloquized:[38]

> Is the Black Tea trade fast leaving Shanghai, and are there influences at work which threaten to deprive us even of Green Tea? . . . It is to Foochow [Fuzhou] we must look for the injury our trade has already sustained . . . The ancient trade at Canton may indeed somewhat revive, but our superior geographical position . . . [should] remove all serious apprehension . . . Foochow however enjoys advantages which can neither be gainsaid nor overcome . . . Teas [can] be conveyed to Foochow at an expense of at least 15 percent less than if conveyed to Shanghai . . .

For this high-minded Shanghai merchant, the solution was not a revocation of the IMCS or a return to the unrecorded trade and contraband phase which followed the Small Sword Rebellion. Rather, he demanded that the other four ports also embrace IMCS regulation – a course of action followed soon afterwards. He deemed such institutionalized abrogation of Chinese tariff autonomy necessary, because " . . . China bound itself by treaty to levy certain duties at all the ports alike . . . [but] ten years' experience has proved the utter inability of a purely Chinese establishment to effect this end – such is the indifference, imbecility and corruption of the race".[39]

The IMCS aside, there are complex reasons why Fuzhou eventually remained a marginal port compared with Shanghai and Guangzhou. Suffice it to say here that Fuzhou (as well as Xiamen) had derived some of their importance during the 1880s not just from tea exports but also from the Taiwanese sugar trade, as well as from rapidly expanding maritime links with overseas Chinese trading communities in Southeast Asia.[40] However, these were severely curtailed after Japan occupied Taiwan in 1895.

As for Ningbo, international trade going through that port was 'dull' right from the outset despite Urmston's prognosis. The main factor here is *not* that Ningbo was in any way at a location inferior to Shanghai's. If anything, Ningbo proffered better deep-water access, was closer to some silk-growing areas and was the hometown of many of Shanghai's prominent Chinese merchants.[41]

Ningbo's falling-behind probably had a lot more to do with the fact that Alcock politically entrenched Shanghai as Britain's most important bastion in China, and was seen as the most able of the British Consuls by far. This meant that most British gunboats in East Asia continued to dock in Shanghai by default, so that the city was perceived by Chinese and foreigners alike as the safest of the five open ports. In addition, Alcock's espousal of the IMCS meant that, in addition to its small mercantile and missionary community, Shanghai's foreign settlement began attracting a bureaucratic work-force as of the mid-1850s. Thus, a complex set of circumstances – a fiscal windfall, consular proactivity, vigorous law enforcement, takeover of tariffs, land-rights grab as well as a good deal of happen-stance – all add up to geography in explaining Shanghai's rise to prominence.

Alcock's consular proactivity is perhaps the most difficult to capture in comparative terms. It can perhaps be best described in reference to how the Taiping Rebellion was handled – the Taipings having been perceived as a much more ominous threat to the foreign community than the Small Swordsmen. The British maintained neutrality in the conflict, though European arms dealers and merce-naries served both the Qing and the Rebels. When the Taipings approached the 'Native City' in February 1862, French gunboats repelled the 'sanguinary wretches' with Alcock's support.[42] Yet, a few months earlier, when the much smaller foreign community at Ningbo had besought Alcock's help in confronting the Taipings, he evaded their pleas. Consequently, Ningbo was brutally run over.[43]

This chapter has suggested that some aspects of Shanghai's history may still be somewhat misunderstood despite an explosion of pertinent studies in recent years, and amid a burgeoning tendency in Western historiography of late imperial China to shift the focus of attention onto other parts of the country.

The primary aspect explored here was the geographical one, namely, the degree to which its location at the mouth of the Yangtze River accounts for Shanghai's rapid early treaty-port development. Shanghai's location was framed as one of a number of important factors that laid the groundwork for the city's rise to prominence as of the 1880s. While leaving the subsequent era of urban growth to future research, discussion in this chapter did underscore fiscal expansion and Alcock's consular proactivity in the 1860s as two factors that merit scholars' closer attention. By way of counter-factual argumentation, it was shown that Shanghai's location had posed at first as many obstacles to development as advantages. Zhoushan, Ningbo and Fuzhou had offered equally – if not more compelling – advantageous geographical features.

To begin with, trade had been the lifeblood of the British Empire, and its stewards quite naturally sought to expand it into China's interior. For centuries, Britain's China trade had been confined to Canton and monopolized by the EIC. The dissolution of the EIC's monopoly in 1834 impelled many to eye northern ports closer to the fabled Yangtze Delta, where much of China's wealth and commodities were produced. Steam technology and superior military capability enabled the British to impose on Imperial China the opening up of four additional ports following the first Opium War.

Few Britons had heard of Shanghai in the 1830s. However, Lindsay's *Amherst* mission – one of the last to explore the North-China coast ports prior to the Opium War – had much praise for Shanghai's potential, to the extent that H.M. Government eventually traded off its interest in Zhoushan for Shanghai (and Hong Kong) around the Nanjing Treaty negotiating table.

That being the case, Shanghai still had to vie with Fuzhou and Canton for mercantile supremacy. It gained the upper hand not only by virtue of its location further up the coast but because of its sound institutional foundation, which was underpinned by a broader fiscal base, comprising hundreds of thousands of wealthy Jiangnan Chinese. These were, in turn, drawn to Shanghai's foreign settlement because of its demonstrable immunity to late-Imperial upheavals.

In that sense, an efficient municipal police backed up by gunboat deterrence was an essential prerequisite for early development. So was Sino-Foreign co-habitation. Upon this solid foundation, the British-run settlement could later improve road infrastructure and port facilities, paving the way for industrialization by the turn of the 19th century. But what if the British had insisted on Zhoushan? Or if the great bulk of their naval force had permanently cast anchor in Ningbo rather than Shanghai in 1843? The end result might well have been equally spectacular, with just as many Jiangnan literati heading in Ningbo's direction.

## Notes

1 Esherick (2002), p. xi.
2 Rogaski (2004); Dikötter (2007).
3 See for example Du (2006); Bickers (2007); Goodman (2009); Henriot (2009).
4 Denison and Guan (2006), p. 56.
5 Gamble (2003), p. xii; Wasserstrom (2009), p. 2; Bergère (2002), p. 32.
6 Cohen (1984).
7 Bickers (1999), pp. 39–40; Wasserstrom (2009), pp. 21–61.
8 Johnson (1995), p. 264.
9 Xiong et al. (1999), vol. 1, 2; Henriot et al. (1999).
10 Lindsay (1843); Gützlaff (1833); Medhust (1838). Frederick Pigou, who was an EIC Director, noted Shanghai's potential as early as 1756.
11 Johnson (1995), pp. 182–185.
12 Fairbank (1953).
13 Wright (1908), Chp. X.
14 Johnson (1995), pp. 212–214.
15 *NCH*, 17 September 1853, p. 26.
16 Quoted in Pott (1928), Chp. X; on the difficulties the Bar posed for Shanghai travellers, see also Cumming (1886), pp. 265–266.
17 Quoted in Pott (1928), Chp. X.
18 Fang 1972; Sun 1990; CFHA (1993).
19 Clark (1921), pp. 6–7.
20 Johnson (1995), p. 343; Lu (1999), p. 36.
21 Lu (1999), pp. 32–35.
22 NCH, 14 January 1854, p. 94.
23 *NCH*, 22 October 1853 and *NCH*, 12 November 1853, *passim*.
24 SMA File U1-1-1293.
25 *NCH*, 8 March 1856, p. 126.
26 *NCH*, 20 January 1855, p. 101.
27 *NCH*, 19 January 1856, p. 99.
28 See e.g. Zhang (1996), p. 41.

29 NCH, 25 May 1856, p. 170.
30 Xiong (1999), vol. 1. For other scholars' work see e.g. Dai (1998), pp. 12–17.
31 Lu (1999), pp. 37–38.
32 Wright (1908), Chp. X.
33 Wright (1908), Chp. X.
34 *NCH*, 31 March 1857, p. 106.
35 Urmston (1834), p. 64; cf. Medhurst's account (1838, pp. 368–369) where "Shang-hae" is described as 'a city of the third-rank [yet] *one of the* greatest emporiums of commerce on the east coast of China. It communicates, immediately, with the rich districts of Soo-chow [Suzhou], and Hang-chow [Hangzhou], receiving the rich brocades from that arcadia of China, and conveying thither, the inventions and commodities of the western world.'
36 On the impact of Lindsay's account on British policy-makers like Lord Palmerston, see e.g. London *Times* Editorial, 28 March 1836, p. 4; see also Denison and Guang, 1999, 32–33. The British relinquishment of Chusan had to do with rumours that the Qing Court would formally cede the island to the French as part of their strategy of pitting 'barbarians' against other 'barbarians'. The British decided to retreat from the island in return for Chinese indemnity, and a promise Chusan would not be ceded to any other European Power. Nonetheless, for many years afterwards, some in the British Foreign Office believed trading Chusan for a 'barren rock' such as Hong Kong had been a grave mistake. For a detailed account, see Beasley (1995), pp. 55–59.
37 *NCH*, 17 June 1854, pp. 182–183.
38 *NCH*, 5 April 1856, pp. 142.
39 *NCH*, 5 April 1856, pp. 142
40 Lindsay (1834, pp. 12–13) described Amoy as a 'celebrated emporium' or a 'flourishing town' that was situated in 'one of the most barren [districts] in China . . . it is dependent on the neighbouring island of Formosa [Taiwan] . . . '. He was more upbeat about Fuzhou (pp. 57–58): ' . . . in point of local and commercial advantages, few cities of the empire are more favourably situated than Fuh Chow . . . Fuh Chow is also a far more central situation than Canton for the distribution of British woollen manufactures, which would also be here in greater request from the coldness of the climate. In the latter point, however, some of the more northern ports, such as Ning-po or Shang-hae, have much greater advantages than Fuh Chow'; Lindsay concluded (pp. 290–291) that expectations that his mission would be allowed to trade were building up the further north it sailed. In Ningbo, local mandarins for the first time even promised him that he would be able to trade upon arrival in Shanghai. Yet, in Shanghai – the northernmost port-of-call – he was snubbed again.

41 Jones (1974); Jones (1976); Brook (1990).
42 *NCH*, 22 February 1862, p. 31.
43 See dispatches from Ningbo in *NCH*, 15 June 1861, p. 94; 15 March 1862, p. 43; and 10 May 1862, p. 75.

# 4

# Re-Examining Public Debt in Republican China, 1912–1937

The conventional view of 1930s Shanghai, entrenched by the victorious Chinese Communist Party two decades later, is that of decadence, corruption and submission to foreigners amid economic depression and bankruptcy of many home-grown industrialists. That attitude is perhaps best epitomized by Mao Dun's celebrated novel *Midnight* where many local protagonists express the view that "... our bankers invest only in KMT government bonds and land"; set in a plotline caricaturing what Mao Dun saw as an obsession with bond speculation, one Chinese owner of a silk filature similarly complained that Shanghainese entrepreneurs were:[1]

> "... attacked from four sides: workers demand higher wages; we're up against competition from Japanese silk in foreign markets; taxes at home are crushing; and the *bankers are stingy* with their loans."

In contrast to Shanghai's foreign-run stock exchange, the great bulk of trade in the city's Chinese-run exchanges was made up of government bonds in the 1930s. In the early 1920s, however, many new Chinese stock exchanges were opened up across the country, and competed with one another. Their trade composition was more variable in nature, but few survived by the end of the decade. That 1920s stock exchange stampede was luridly depicted in the Chinese press at the time. Much of this sensationalist coverage was disapproving of the speculative nature of these new exchanges; it reserved particular venom for the participation of women investors in the trade. In that sense, the coverage presaged Mao Dun's more forceful castigation a decade later, whereby parasitism, bond speculation and vice were seen as mutually reinforcing.[2]

Notably, Shanghai's *foreign*-run bourse was somewhat different to other bourses across the British empire in that British investment in China was small compared with Latin America or Africa, and mostly geared toward finance and shipping sectors before the turn of the 20th century. Banking, insurance and docks therefore made up the bulk of stock capitalization, whilst mining and agricultural stocks were rather small in volume compared with other developing regions.[3]

Since Shanghai's "opening up" as a British treaty port in 1842, fluctuations in the city's financial markets were more often than not driven by regional factors, with global cycles of boom and bust less apparent in local price shares. The main exceptions followed bankruptcy of foreign trading firms: the 1857 American stock crash brought down, for example, Wetmore & Co. and King & Co.; the 1873 financial crisis in Europe led to short-term credit stringency locally; and the famous 1890 collapse of the major merchant bank Baring Brothers indirectly led to the dissolution of Russel & Co.[4]

Similarly, it was the 1895 Shimonoseki Treaty, ending the first Sino-Japanese war, which set off Shanghai's second phase of rapid growth in that it allowed foreigners for the first time not just to reside in treaty-ports but also to actually set up wholly-owned factories on Chinese soil. This was soon translated into more versatile share offering on the local stock exchange, although the volume of industrial stock was still small compared with financials.[5] But in 1910, Shanghai's foreign stock exchange crashed – due, in large part, to fluctuating world rubber prices, compounded by fraudulently-induced *local* overtrading in rubber plantation stock. The crash left scores of Chinese-owned moneyshops insolvent, and foreign banks in the city were weighed down by worthless IOUs; the total outstanding debt of Shanghai moneyshops was estimated at 20 million taels (tael being the traditional unit of account in pre-war Shanghai nominally worth 0.72 silver dollar), and their numbers dropped precipitously form 80 to 36 by 1911. Worse still, the stock exchange crash ramified into a nationwide crisis that crippled nascent railway ventures, and was responsible in part for the provincial discontent that eventually toppled the Qing dynasty. It thereby ushered in the early-Republic (i.e. Beiyang, 1912–1926) era that was characterized by weak central government and regional warlordism.[6]

During World War I, the foreign-run bourse remained opened with few restrictions although share prices slumped considerably;

the war in fact was a boon to East Asian economies provisioning of Europe's war-torn economies with civilian goods. Once the war was over, share prices shot up across all sectors in Shanghai but particularly in the cotton mill sector, which had by then expanded manifold.[7] By 1923, however, the composite Shanghai share index had caught up with its pre-World War I peak. It continued to climb up with an interval of few months on account of the bloody anti-British riots in the city following the 1925 May Thirtieth Incident; nationalist unrest in 1925–6 was not confined to Shanghai, it rapidly spread south and "nearly brought Hong Kong's economy to a halt".[8] Yet, the semi-colonial setting of Shanghai meant that foreign banks there could not enjoy the kind of absolute backing that the colonial authorities in Hong Kong could extend to British banks. The upshot was that from 1925, Shanghai's foreign banks were forced to negotiate with Chinese banks formal admission into their clearing mechanisms, culminating in the setting up of a joint Sino-Foreign Association of Shanghai Banks (February, 1929) and Exchange Brokers' Association (October, 1929).[9]

By and large, however, the *longer*-term upward trend of Shanghai's foreign-run bourse, which started after 1912, did not abate until New York's Black Tuesday (1929) started depressing markets worldwide. In fact, between 1925 and 1929, the Shanghai foreign-run stock exchange diversified further with the vibrant growth of Malayan rubber-plantation offerings driven by world demand for automobile tyres. Because the previous rubber-share exuberance in Shanghai had ended in severe crisis in 1910, however, local investors were now more circumspect – in general shares associated with tyre manufacturing appreciated much less in Shanghai during the 1920s than in other parts of the world.[10]

In that sense, the performance of China's financial markets can arguably be considered more aligned with the rest of the world only *after* 1929. Furthermore, in the early 1930s, the world price of silver started edging above the nominal exchange-value of China's silver-based currency, resulting in the flow of silver from China's hinterland to Shanghai, whence it was often smuggled out of the country. Concomitantly, the inflow of silver-based funds into the city meant "easy money" could be borrowed and poured into the local real estate and stock exchanges.[11]

Pressured by regional mining interests in the Congress, the administration of US President Franklin Delano Roosevelt embarked on its Silver Purchase Policy, designed to lift America out of recession in 1934. One of the immediate side-effects of this policy was that China – now the only country in the world to cling to the silver standard – saw a more rapid erosion in her terms of trade, slashing exports and crippling the industrial base of the treaty-port economy. The implication for China's economy was double-pronged. First, after years of inflation and debasement, China's metallic currency was appreciating artificially on the cross-rates. It made imports cheaper, thus dampening the relative price of agri-cultural produce and hitting living standards in the rural hinterland. But, much more importantly, it made simple business sense to buy silver dollars in Shanghai for US dollars or other foreign currencies and melt them into silver.[12]

Ironically, for three years the silver standard protected the Chinese economy from the worst effects of the World Depression that beclouded the West in 1929. To be sure Chinese traditional exports like silk plummeted due to lower global demand but the appreciation of gold-based currencies meant that expensive imports were pushing up the price of agricultural commodities to the benefit of the rural hinterland.[13] A downturn began to loom on the horizon in 1931–33 when Britain and then the US came off the gold stan-dard. On 19 June 1934 the US Congress passed the Silver Purchase Act in a bid to re-vitalize the silver mining industry and alleviate conditions in several Midwest states. The immediate upshot was a drastic depletion of Chinese silver reserves in favour of much higher prices in the New York and London commodity exchanges. China was thus belatedly drawn into the whirlwind of the Depression.[14]

The preponderance of government bond trade in Shanghai's Chinese-run bourse accentuated once the KMT took over the reins. Notably, after its establishment in 1927, the Nanjing government turned away from reliance on foreign credit. With a few exceptions China had begun defaulting on foreign loans as of the early 1920s. Whilst Chinese bonds backed directly by Maritime Customs Revenue continued to pay interest to foreign investors, by 1939 vritually all Chinese external loans were in default.[15] Instead, the KMT is said to have flooded the Chinese-run stock exchange in Shanghai with high-yield bonds whose proceeds were vital for the KMT's continued military build-up and campaign against regional warlords. In 1934, the Chinese-run bourse relocated to a purpose built eight-storey edifice on 422 Hankou Road. in the International Settlement, but the main bulk of its trade continued to be in KMT bonds. After the outbreak of the second Sino-Japanese war in 1937, the KMT's reliance on bond issuance and bank loans became yet more pronounced.[16]

Between 1927 and 1935, domestic debt mainly floated as government bonds totalled more than 1.6 billion silver dollars, compared with a total of only 612 million dollars in the previous 15 years of the Beiyang governments' tenure (1912–1927). Mao Dun's invective and other contemporary sources suggest that most of these bonds had in fact been taken up in advance by Chinese-run banks, rather than traded diffusely by individual investors. These bonds, it is often alleged, crowded out what little trade emerged in Chinese private equity. Only about 2% of Chinese stock exchange capitalization was attributable to non-government corporate securities during the early 1930s. However, more recent sources suggest that the onset of the Pacific War in 1937 meant the KMT power in Shanghai was eclipsed, and it could therefore hardly find buyers for its new debentures there. Thus, Chinese industrialists are said to have enjoyed more breathing space, and were able to mobilize capital more readily in Shanghai capital markets thereafter.[17]

Accordingly, the common perception of the 1930s is that, in the absence of attractive home-grown corporate stock offerings, Chinese investors' capital fuelled the growth of a foreign bourse that rarely listed Chinese joint-stock companies in the strict sense of the word. Similarly, Shanghai expatriates did not invest in a Chinese bourse that was little more than an instrument for floating *domestic* public debt – Chinese governments pledged substantive collateral security only against the *foreign* debt that foreign banks helped them float in the London capital market.[18]

## Public Debt Crowding Out Industrialization?

The entrenched notion that speculation in bonds was the bane of Shanghai pre-war finance is supported, to some extent, by Liu Zhiying's important 2004 study. Liu was not able to re-construct a time series of trade patterns in the city's Chinese-run bourse but, based on painstaking research at the Shanghai Municipal Archives, came to the conclusion that much of the activity there after 1928 revolved around KMT public debt. He estimated the volume of trade in 1931 at $3.7 billion, a total equivalent to just 2.3 times the amount of KMT government debt floated hitehrto.[19]

In order to control the Chinese-run bourse, the KMT eliminated diffuse trade, and created one venue for floor bidding on Hankou Rd. Prior to 1937, Chinese investors sceptical of the government's ability to honour its bonds were drawn to Shanghai's foreign-run stock exchange, set up as early as 1891. Like its Chinese equivalents, this foreign bourse was often buffeted by speculative bubbles – but it managed to weather fleeting storms and grow fast in the early 20th century. By 1905, the foreign bourse in Shanghai was incorporated under Hong Kong law, primarily listing expatriate treaty-port firms and municipal utilities, tobacco and rubber plantations, coal mines and cotton mills.[20]

As early as 1872, the British-run Shanghai Municipal Council [SMC], the governing body, of the International Settlement, had issued its first tranche of bonds in the foreign-run bourse, offering 8% interest p.a. Subsequent floatations were made every year, and grew increasingly bigger. A few years later, the French Settlement municipal council followed suit with a floatation of its own. These two councils' bonds were enthusiastically taken up by the expatriate community. For example, when prominent Baghdadi-Jewish Shanghai businessman Sir Ellis Kadoorie died in 1922, it emerged that he had in his possession no less than 106,500 taels (hereafter, Tls) worth of Shanghai municipal-council debentures out of some Tls 376,175 in local securities (including corporate shares).[21] Similarly, Tycho Wing was a prominent British lawyer residing in Shanghai; from his estate it emerges that upon his death in 1935 he held Tls 8,252 in French-council debentures out of a total of Tls 29,675 in securities (including corporate shares).[22]

By the 1920s, SMC annual bonds offerings had already made up around third of new SMC liabilities. The reason why the two foreign-run municipal councils increasingly took to bonds was simple: right from their establishment over half of municipal council income relied on Chinese rate-payers and licence fees paid in largely by Chinese-run businesses. Since these rates and fees were relatively hard to collect, and required an ever larger enforcement mechanism, bonds proved an attractive means of gaining cheap credit for capital works like dredging and utilities, which ensured the foreign Settlements' reputation as the most modern places in China at the time. That reputation, grounded as it was on superior entrepôt infrastructure, meant in turn that Shanghai also became the most desirable place to live in China. So much so that in 1910, a few expatriates actually accused the SMC of crowding out investment in local corporate shares by soaking up all the available capital with their bond issues. In other words, the notion that bonds crowded out corporate share trading was by no means limited to Chinese industrialists indignant at the KMT's heavy hand.[23] Moreover, in Hong Kong, where the British had more administrative leverage, industrialization was by and large discouraged prior to 1949 precisely so as to preserve the colony's entrepôt character, and pre-empt competition from local manufacturers to British imports.[24]

Shanghai debenture issues listed on the local-foreign bourse were annually compiled in the *China Stock and Share Handbook*. The data for 1917, for example, would indeed confirm that the great bulk of these issue were made by the two foreign-run municipal councils, followed by local utilities, local hotels, local department stores, overseas rubber estates, local realty firms and local race clubs. Not a single industrial venture seems to have substantively raised capital through debenture issuance on Shanghai's foreign-run bourse up to that point.[25] The data for 1926 do not evince radical change except for the listing of important new Chinese-run financial institutions like, for example, the privately-owned Kiangsu Bank (incorp. 1912), the Kincheng Bank (see below), and the Yien-Yieh Commercial Bank (incorp. 1914). There were five Chinese-run industrial firms principally listed that year: The Chee Hsin Cement Company; the Chiu Ta Salt Company; Der Ah Wing & Co.; the Lih The Oil Mill and the Nanyang Brothers Tobacco Co.[26]

On the other hand, one would need to recall that most utility companies operating in Shanghai's two foreign settlements were subsidiaries of metropole consortia which had raised their capital mainly in the West. They were, in that sense, different to Chinese-run utility companies operating in the city's other precincts within the KMT's direct or indirect reach. Since KMT bonds were preponderant in the Chinese-run bourse, these Chinese-run companies often relied on credit from local branches of British and Japanese banks.[27]

Shanghai further distinguished itself from other treaty-ports by a more extensive tramway system. A British-registered firm, the Shanghai Electric Construction Co., was for example set up to that end in 1914 with a paid-in capital of US$1.68 million. US utility firms jumped into the local fray only a decade later, but from then on many local European subsidiaries were concerned of being taken over by American firms.[28] By 1937, American & Foreign Power Co. (A&FP) was the largest global electricity provider, holding assets valued at US$ 534.6 million. Although not even partly listed on the Shanghai bourse, and without much business in the French settlement, which was zealously guarded for French firms, A&FP's subsidiary became the biggest power company in China. Because of this, the net capitalization of the foreign-run bourse in Shanghai actually understated the amount of business conducted there.[29]

Listings by the *China Stock and Share Handbook* for 1913 show for example, that while some local utility companies nominated their paid-in capital in silver dollars or Tls, some others nominated foreign currency for that purpose – arguably suggesting limited share-trade activity locally. Thus, the British-run Shanghai Electric Construction Co. (incorp. in 1905) had paid-in capital of GBP 320,000 in 1913, while the Shanghai Gas Company had Tls 2.5 million in paid in capital that year. Curiously, the Raub Australian Gold Mines also appeared in the Shanghai listing with GBP 200,000 in paid-in capital. [30] Notably, as early as 1913, what were probably two Chinese-run industrial ventures also made the principal listing: The Laou Kung Mow Cotton Spinning and Weaving Co. (incorporated 1895) with Tls 800,000; and Soy Chee Cotton Spinning Co. (incorp. 1895) with Tls 1 million.[31]

Generally, Chinese investors' money fuelled the growth of a foreign bourse that rarely listed Chinese joint-stock companies in the strict sense of the word. Similarly, Shanghai expatriates did not invest in a Chinese bourse that was little more than an instrument for floating *domestic* public debt. As already mentioned, Chinese governments pledged substantive collateral security only against the *foreign* debt that foreign banks helped them float in the London capital market. Why didn't the SMC push for a more integrative equity market comprising both Chinese and expatriate-run firms? For the SMC to have acted along these lines and run the risk of rankling Beijing or Nanjing – explicit fiscal incentives would be required. However, before the mid-1920s Chinese residents of the International (and French) Concession had been willing to pay rates even without executive representation on the SMC and French council, if only to protect their wealth from government exactions. At the same time, taxpayers in Britain – rather than expatriate SMC ratepayers – shouldered most of Shanghai's onerous defense outlay.[32]

As portrayed by Mao Dun, one of the most serious allegations voiced by Chinese economists, as from the 1920s, was that insufficient bank credit to local entrepreneurs impeded China's industrialization. What is more, recent studies have shown that *Chinese*-owned banks were ready, in turn, to lend to *foreign* firms at lower-interest.[33]

To date, no comprehensive attempt has been made to juxtapose the ethnic and sectorial makeup of British bank liabilities and assets in Shanghai. Similarly, we do not know the exact volume of foreign bank shares subscribed by ethnic Chinese, so as to compare it with Chinese boardroom representation, or their share of staff remuneration.[34] On the other hand, comprehensive surveys of small and medium-size Chinese industrial ventures in pre-war Shanghai clearly suggest that very few had initially relied on bank loans – let alone foreign bank loans – in the *early* stages of organization.[35]

Indeed, a cursory overview of principal share price listings in the Shanghai English-language press suggests that Chinese-bourse corporate shares were hardly ever mentioned, while early-Republican and KMT government bonds floated in London and locally made an entry only occasionally. By far, much more coverage was devoted to share and bond prices as quoted on the foreign-run bourse. Yet, before the turn of the 20th century, such share listings rarely featured industrial corporate shares be they Chinese or foreign sounding – the Shanghai Brick & Saw Mill Co. was perhaps the most notable exception. Foreign-run utilities like the Shanghai Gas Co. or French-run Compagnie du Gaz, by comparison, were listed locally as early as 1864–5.[36]

## How Much KMT Debt Was Taken Up by Chinese Banks?

Marie-Claire Bergère famously advanced the characterization of the early 1920s as the *golden age* of prewar Shanghai. The breakdown of central government, coupled with a depreciation of China's silver currency, strengthened local manufacturers. During and immediately following World War I, local manufacturing could compete with imported goods and services on improved terms of trade and free of government exactions. This relative freedom was conducive to business, as the resources of foreign powers were being mobilized for the war effort in Europe. However, in the early 1930s – we are told – local Chinese enterprises were buffeted by KMT extortion, and then adversely affected by the winds of the Great Depression. Through much of this period, a resurgent central government –

established by the KMT in Nanjing – swamped money markets with discounted bonds and effectively nationalized large banks.[37]

Insightful as it was, Bergère's classic argument was grounded for the most part in qualitative observations. More recent quantitative research into the city's prewar economy yields conclusions that are far less decisive. There is a clear gap, for example, between Bergère's and Linsun Cheng's understanding of the so-called Shanghai golden age, its duration, or the KMT's role therein. According to Cheng's path-breaking quantitative analysis, privately-run banks continued to prosper in Shanghai well into the 1930s. His revisionist claim is that government-bond acquisition (lending to the KMT government, in other words) was *not* the mainstay of Shanghai banks and scarcely affected the overall business climate at the time. Such a proposition immediately invites greater attention from business historians in view of a growing body of work that is now seeking to *rehabilitate* the Republican era more broadly.[38]

Cheng Linsun, in a sense, problematized the conventional view, entrenched by Mao Dun, that Chinese banks did not lend enough to home-grown industrial ventures because they preferred to lend to the KMT in the 1930s. In his exhaustive 2007 study, Hong Jiaguan similarly showed that bond holding by Chinese banks was indeed dominated by KMT securities but, overall, these did not make up much more than 10%–18% of individual Chinese bank secured loan portfolios (mostly in the form of credit to the KMT against KMT securities as collateral).[39] However, Hong and – perhaps somewhat more explicitly – Sheehan do nevertheless suggest that the KMT crowding out of credit to industrial entrepreneurs might have occurred through unsecured bank loans to the government rather than just by bonds *per se*.[40]

Chinese scholarship on pre-war banking was until recently supportive of this view: important evidence from the Bank of Communications (*Jiaotong yinhang*), one of the main four government banks at the time, was compiled for example in 1995, with commentary stating that the Beiyang government annually borrowed from this bank between 30–40 million silver dollars, or approximately half of the total credit the bank advanced. Though in November 1928 the KMT government re-designated the Bank of Communications as China's leading provider of industrial-credit, it *also* borrowed heavily from this bank toward non-industrial ends. In 1933, such loans to the KMT stood at 20 million silver dollars, making up no less than 60% of the credit advanced by the bank that year. At the same time, the Bank's banknote issuance expanded commensurately.[41]

In what follows, I argue that the gap between Cheng, Hong and Sheenan's interpretation may, indeed, be partly reconciled by a closer look at Chinese bank note issuance. By the early 1930s, most Chinese banks of issue were amenable to the KMT government. Perceived government backing helped them disburse more and more notes in the hinterland. China at that time was on a silver standard, but the question that needs to be posed in this context is whether bank reserves held against note issuance were purely metallic.

To be sure, KMT edicts nominally obligated Chinese banks of issue to hold 100% backing against notes in circulation, but only 60% of that reserve was mandated as metallic by necessity. Theoretically, then, Chinese banks of issue could secure at least 40% of their banknote issue by holding *different* forms of KMT debt quite apart from acquiring KMT bonds in the open market.[42]

How thoroughly were the reserve edicts followed? As indicated, the answer to this question might have much broader implications for our understanding of the period. Concomitantly, this question invites more extensive research into extant bank ledgers. Yet, extant balance-sheet data from the larger Chinese banks of issue are, perhaps intentionally, opaque. In other words, it is exceedingly difficult to match asset and liability entries, let alone to re-construct the composition of the reserves held against notes in circulation at the time. For these reason, data from smaller banks of issue can be instructive.

Liu Yongxiang's 2006 important study, for example, examined the Kincheng Banking Corporation (*Jincheng yinhang* 金城銀行). Because of its characteristics, this bank is highly pertinent to the question posed above: set up in 1917, and headquartered in Tianjin, Kincheng accounted for as much as 4% of all Chinese bank deposits at the time. More importantly, the bank was from the outset promoted by the Beiyang government, which nominally ruled China between the fall of the Qing dynasty in 1912, and the KMT's sweep to power in 1927. Partially in tune with Cheng Linsun and Hong Jiaguan's findings, Liu found that in the early Republican era (1912–1927), total deposits in Chinese-run banks accounted for just 10.9% of all deposits in 1921. In other words, the home-grown banking sector was by far smaller than the overall size of foreign banks operating in China even when it came to retail activity. Yet, under KMT auspices, the share of deposits in Chinese-run banks had climbed to no less than 17.3% (i.e. 475 million silver dollars) by 1934.[43]

Parsing in-house ledgers, Liu Yongxiang came to the conclusion that, quite apart from holding Beiyang government bonds, as much as 31.12% of Kincheng bank's loans (some 1.7 million silver dollars) were advanced to various Beiyang-affiliated warlords and officials in 1919. By contrast, in 1937 only 10.7% of total Kincheng loans that year (10.3 million silver dollars) could be attributed to KMT-affiliated interests. However, KMT-issued bonds made up as much as 71.85% of all bond holdings by the Kincheng bank that year; 26.71% was made up of foreign-currency denominated bonds, suggesting perhaps local municipal-council debentures or British consoles. Only 0.01% of Kincheng bank's bond holding that year could be attributed to Chinese corporate issues.[44]

These Kincheng indicators can perhaps be better evaluated when compared with whatever data is available from the Shanghai head-quarters of the Bank of China [BoC], a nominally privately-owned institution but one that was in time designated by the KMT as one of China's principal banks of issue. In 1914, for example, the Shanghai headquarters accounted for only 17.2% of total BoC notes in circulation. But by 1928 – only a year into the KMT's rule – Shanghai's share had already reached 65%.[45]

In 1928 the BoC's headquarters advanced two short-term loans to the KMT totalling 1.9 milllion silver dollars. By comparison, over the course of 1930 the headquarters advanced no fewer than 26 such short-term loans, totalling 23.3 million silver dollars in all, or nearly 10% of the BoC's total Shanghai balance-sheet that year. Extant records are not always revealing, but based on balance-sheet juxtaposition it would appear that these short-term loans were largely unsecured. In other words, it is likely that such loans added onto direct KMT liabilities in the form of bonds rather than consti-tuted a part thereof. However, at best, only a third of BoC's Shanghai balance-sheet total can be attributed to KMT govern-ment-related business, suggesting that the BoC was much more than merely a channel for offloading KMT debt, as previous studies might have led us to believe. In other words, the picture that emerges from both Kincheng and BoC ledgers is more complex than what conventional wisdom might entail, laying out a middle-ground between Bergère's pessimism about the nature of Chinese banking under KMT auspices, and Cheng Linsun's emphasis on the vitality and independence of this sector through the 1930s.[46]

Where the foregoing survey might go slightly beyond Bergère's and Cheng's classic work is in calling attention to the fact that banknote issuance remained a critical function of institutions like the BoC under both Beiyang and KMT rule. Yet, banknote issuance took up a slightly smaller share of BoC operations in Shanghai during the Nanjing decade (1927–1937) than under Beiyang auspices, a fact that might lend additional credence to Cheng's assessment of the sector. Be that as it may, BoC ledgers tell us too little about the composition of note reserves to reach conclusive findings. Though the reserve was meant to be 100% by law, other ledger entries suggest the volume of specie and bullion in the Bank's vaults rarely amounted to more than 10% of the volume of notes in circulation. Pending further archival evidence, it is not clear precisely what kind of assets made the bulk of note reserves, and to what extent KMT various forms of debt underpinned an expansion of note issuance.[47]

From 1927, when the KMT came to power, to 1936, just before the Pacific war started, cash reserves (broadly defined) rarely made more than 20% of volume of notes in circulation on the BoC's Shanghai ledger. This is an important indicator not least because Shanghai accounted for only about a tenth of BoC's total note issuance across the country in the 1910s; it then made up over a third of BoC's total note issuance in the 1920s, and over a half in the 1930s.[48]

Based on these data, even if one were to allow for a higher-end estimate of 50% as the share which KMT bonds and note reserves took up on the asset-side in Shanghai – it would still be difficult to explain the remaining 50% in terms of the exact nature of BoC operations in the 1930s. One might be tempted to assume that the other half represented other forms of KMT collateral provided against credit transfers – collateral that was obscurely registered on the liability side. But merely weighing up relative shares would block out a good deal of what transpired at the time: in absolute terms, the BoC's Shanghai note circulation figures shot up exponentially from merely 2.8 million silver dollars in 1914 to a whopping 294 million silver dollars by 1936. In other words, the Shanghai headquarters experienced a hundred-fold increase in notes outstanding between the Beiyang period and the Nanjing decade. Where were the metallic proceeds of the exponential growth in banknote issuance forwarded? It would appear that future scholarship on Republican China ought to address this question as a priority if we are to reach a clearer picture of the country's pre-war economy. More extensive archival work in that vein seems long overdue.

Mao Dun's narrative is not only germane to the pre-war era. Prior to 1991, the perceived predatory nature of KMT policy in Shanghai was often compared with the CCP's policy of turning Shanghai into Socialism's fiscal "milch cow. Both KMT and CCP policies were seen as inflating government and emaciating civil society in stark contrast to the minimalist government bureaucracy and gentry voluntarism that defined Qing governance. On the other hand, the PRC's ascendancy on the world stage nowadays is conspicuously devoid of massive domestic debt floatations, and since 1991 Shanghai has been enjoying preferential treatment from Beijing. Yet, even today the Shanghai stock exchange is often seen as 'rigged' by the state.[49] In that sense, it is important to more clearly distinguish between KMT- and PRC-run Shanghai, and stimulate further debate on the city's pre-war legacy among historians and contemporary China watchers.

This chapter reprised classic and more recent studies of pre-war Shanghai's economy in a bid to re-examine the widely-held notion that Shanghainese banks and industrialists were often held to ransom. The notion that the KMT neutered home-grown capital markets and forestalled industrialization with excessive issue of bonds taken up by subservient banks of issue may be partly valid, but it should not remain unqualified in view of more recent studies. For, as discussed here, expatriates also complained at times about excessive bond issues by the city's *foreign*-run councils. On the other hand, much of Shanghai's corporate economy and infrastructure was actually listed elsewhere due to the semi-colonial nature of the city. Thus, total corporate stock listed in the city's bourses at the time understated the significance of joint-stock entreprise vis-à-vis KMT or municipal securities.

In other words, the issue at hand must not be simplistically boiled down to KMT malignance. After all, KMT monetary policy did prove enormously successful in strengthening the home-grown banking sector. Neither was Shanghai uniquely under-industrialized: in fact it had become one of the *most* industrialized localities in East Asia on the eve of the Pacific War. Nevertheless, circumstantial evidence does suggest that, unlike Shanghai's foreign-run bourse, corporate share and debenture floatations were rare on the Chinese-run bourse. Chinese-language media reports from the time do often reinforce Mao Dun's castigation of the speculative nature of the Chinese bourse in the mid-1920s to the 1930s, and are particularly disapproving of female investor morality. Shanghai had already become at the time China's most industrial hub, and industrial ventures were far from being confined to the foreign sector even if Chinese entrepreneurs mostly raised start-up fund through means other than share floatations.[50]

Fluctuations on both the Chinese and foreign-run bourses were affected by local and regional factors as least as much they were affected by the prevailing mood in Western bourses. But the fact that China was the only major country to remain on a silver currency after 1930, as world silver prices were appreciating, meant that it would now feel the full brunt of the Great Depression, and demand for Chinese industrial goods would slump. Yet, in the early 1930s, the ultimate outflow of silver from China meant that much funds had to be brought to Shanghai in the first instance, thereby creating a realty bubble even as the city's industrial sector was in strife.

The complex circumstances of 1930s call for more detailed studies in the future. At the very least, it would appear that Marie-Claire Bergère's thesis of the early 1920s as the *golden age* of prewar Shanghai may need slight revision in view of the fact that some sectors of the city's economy – not least, banking – continued to prosper well into the 1930s. To be sure, Bergère's insight about the inimical aspects of KMT reliance on bonds and its predatory nature in dealing with the city's business elite might remain incontrovertible for the most part. Yet, more recent archival work suggests that bond speculation took up a much smaller share of Chinese bank operations in the city than Mao Dun's *Midnight* might lead us to believe. More important were the Chinese banks' ability to exponentially increase their monetary emissions in the 1930s over and above the volume prevalent during the Beiyang era (1912–1927). It is hoped that these discursive themes will be further elucidated by students of the period in the years to come, particularly as regards the composition of note reserves in Chinese banks during the 1930s, and putative links between bond holdings and annual profits.

## Notes

1 Mao (trans. 1957), Chapter 2, p. 43. *Italics* added by the author. 'Bankers are Stingy' is rendered from the somewhat more sedate original: 金融界對于放款又不肯通融, or "financiers are unwilling to hand out loans".

2 Goodman (2005, 2009).

3 Hao (1986), pp. 355. Notably, three decades later, Lieu (1929, pp. 115–117, tables 39, 40) estimated *real* British investment in China at 1.4 billion silver dollars with manufacturing accounting for as much as 603 million; insurance accounted for 301.5 million; realty, 97 million; and banking 72 million. At the same time, Lieu estimated Japanese investment in China at 1.2 billion silver dollars, which were mainly concentrated in cotton mills shipping and banks. Yet, it may be the case that Lieu's figure for British manufacturing investment was exaggerated, not least because the manufacturing sector was fairly marginal on the Shanghai foreign-run bourse.

4 Hao (1986), pp. 323–324; Liu (2004), pp. 34–41.

5 Rowe (2010), pp. 234–236; Honig (1992), pp. 16–26; Thomas (2001), p. 136.

6 McElderry (1976), pp. 111–115; Du (2002), pp. 85–87; Thomas (2001), pp. 145–169; Bergère (1964), pp. 1–11.

7 Brown (1989).

8 Carroll (2007), pp. 99–101. Cf. Miners (1987), pp. 16–19; Waldron, (1995), p. 244; Carroll (2007), pp. 99–101; Tsang (2007), pp. 92–98. Cf. Chan (2009), pp. 23–27.

9 He (2003).

10 Thomas (2001), pp. 191–198.

11 Shiroyama (2008), pp. 146–148.

12 Friedman and Schwartz (1963), pp. 483–492.

13 See Lin (1935), *passim.*

14 Sheehan (2003), p. 163; some scholars have argued that US silver policy did not affect China's economy radically – see the debate between Friedman (1992), Brandt and Sargeant (1989) and Rawski (1993).

15 Goetzmann, Ukhov and Zhu (2007), p. 280.

16 Goetzmann, Ukhov and Zhu (2007), p. 283. For a photo of this now defunct stock-exchange building, see http://www.news365.com.cn/wxpd/bhygb/shzd/200904/t20090413_2279681.htm [Accessed 9 November 2013].

17 McElderry (2001), pp. 9–10; Lieu (1936), p. 158; Hong Jiaguan (1989), pp. 147–147; Liu Zhiying (2004, pp. 29, 180–190, table 3.4) estimated the value of all Chinese corporate bond issues between 1914–1936 at a mere 41.3 million silver dollars.

18 Paauw (1950); Chen (1965). cf. Thomas (1984).

19 Liu (2004), pp. 24, 163.
20 Hong (1989), pp. 136–137; Thomas (2001), pp. 35–38 , 86–91; Zhu (1989), p. 38.
21 Kadoorie's probate files are held at the UK National Archives, FO 917/2315.
22 UK National Archives, FO 917/3459.
23 Thomas (2001), pp. 60, 84–85. In 1919, Tls 1,034,000 worth of debentures were issued by the SMC. Out of this total, no less than Tls 313,700 worth were taken up by Chinese residents.
24 Carroll (2007), 93; cf. Tsang (2007), p. 108.
25 See the periodical *China Stock and Share Handbook* (1917), pp. 64–65. For and overview of utility companies in China at that time (dockyards, electricity, gas, telephony, tramways, waterworks), see also the periodical *List of the Principal Foreign and Chinese Industrial Enterprises in China and Hong Kong* (1918), pp. 13–20, 24–25, 54–56, 57–59.
26 See the periodical *China Stock and Share Handbook* (1926), *passim*.
27 Lieu (1929) pp. 98–99.
28 As a measure of the relative size of British real investment worldwide, it is worth noting that while the Shanghai Electric Construction Co. which laid out the city's tram system was capitalized at the equivalent of US$ 1.6 million only, the Bombay Electric Supplies & Tramways was capitalized at US$9.8. See Hausman, Hertner and Wilkins (2008), pp. 106–107, table 3.1, pp. 156–161, 189.
29 Hausman, Hertner and Wilkins (2008), p. 218, table 5.1, p. 391, footnote 140.
30 *China Stock and Share Handbook* (1913), pp. 48–49, 81.
31 *China Stock and Share Handbook* (1913), pp. 147, 149.
32 On Chinese ratepayers' campaign for representation on the SMC – see Kotenev (Rep. 1968), pp. 40–44. cf. Johnstone (Rep. 1937), pp. 226–243.
33 See e.g. *China's First Modern Bank* (1982), p. 142; Ishii (2002), pp. 122–124.
34 In that context, Thomas (2001, pp. 80–81, 88) suggests, for example, that Chinese employees owned at least 413 shares of the 40,000 shares issued by HSBC upon its inception.
35 For proponents of this view – see Zhang (1936), pp. 315–317. Cf. *Machine-Manufacturing Entrepreneurship in Pre-War Shanghai* (1979), *passim*; Elvin (2008).
36 Thomas (2001), p. 48. Notably, the Shanghai Electricity Co. lit up the Bund as early as 1883. But it had experienced finance difficulties right from the beginning. By 1892, it was bought out by the Shanghai Municipal Council and remained in public hands right until 1929.
37 Bergère (1986); cf. Bergère (2009), pp. 147–176.
38 Cheng Linsun (2003); for the "rehabilitation" of the Republican era

more broadly, see e.g., Wakeman and Edmonds, eds. (2000); Dikötter (2008).
39 Cheng (2003); Hong (2003), pp. 121–125.
40 Sheehan (2003); Hong (2003), p. 123) stresses that the success of Chinese bank note issuance derived in part from the fact that larger KMT-backed banks enticed smaller banks to disburse the former's notes to clients over the counter by agreeing to supply notes to smaller-bank in return for non-cash securities of up to 60% of the value of notes supplied. These securities, in turn, often represented indirect loans to the KMT. When supplied, such notes (*lingyong chaopiao*領用鈔票) bore the larger-bank insignia but also contained a secret identifier that helped the larger banks trace notes presented to them by clients for encashment to the smaller bank implicated. Thus, larger banks could reduce smaller-bank assets in their ledger whenever notes came a full circle. See also *Jiu Shanghai de jinrongjie* (988), pp. 187–190.
41 *Historic Materials from the Bank of Communications* (1995), vol. I, pp. 349–350, 358–362.
42 Cheng (2003), p. 167. Cf. *Historic Materials from the Bank of Communications* (1995), vol. II, pp. 805–975.
43 Liu (2006), pp. 71–78.
44 Liu (2006), pp. 79–80.
45 *History of the Bank of China's Shanghai Branch* (1991), p. 22.
46 *History of the Bank of China's Shanghai Branch* (1991), p. 62.
47 *History of the Bank of China's Shanghai Branch* (1991), p. 230, tables 1–2.
48 See Rawski (1989), p. 371, table C2.
49 Chen (2007).
50 See e.g. *Machine-Manufacturing Entrepreneurship in Pre-War Shanghai* (1979), vol. I, pp. 459–466; *Rubber-Industry Entrepreneurship in Pre-War Shanghai* (1979), pp. 85–114.

# 5

# Past Glory, Present Hopes

The PRC is arguably more open today that it has ever been in its history, and Shanghai is the face with which it has chosen to project this openness to the outside world more than any other city. As mentioned earlier, the Shanghai Municipal Archives, Shanghai Academy of Social Sciences Archive and Zikawei Library have all undergone digitization with much of their rare English and French documentary material made available in JPG or microfilm form. Better still, even some hitherto inaccessible municipal records from the 1950s and 1960s have now been placed in the public domain.[1]

The availability of these records is already making its mark on new important Western studies of the city's pre-war history, as Mark Swislocki's ground-breaking *Culinary Nostalgia* clearly shows.[2] Yet signals of possibly greater openness as regards more topical materials are mixed at best: whilst many satellite channels are beaming popular-science, history, news and commentary from independent sources to Shanghainese subscribers – BBC World is banned and others face repeated blackouts. This is perhaps instructive when compared with Iran. There, BBC World's new Farsi satellite channel was widely and readily accessible at least until the disputed general elections, which led to Mahmoud Ahmadinejad's reinstatement.[3]

In the realm of corporate business, both 'big' and 'small', the local authorities are also sending mixed message. On the one hand, in May 2009, it was announced with much fanfare that select foreign companies like Australian resource giant Fortescue Metals or the now UK-based HSBC would soon be allowed to list on the Shanghai Stock Exchange, hitherto known for its lack of transparency and preponderance of non-tradable State-Owned Enterprise (SOEs) stock.[4] The announcement was designed to raise Shanghai's profile as a budding global finance centre keener than ever to attract foreign investment and expertise. Yet in what could perhaps be interpreted as reversal of the very same policy, Rio Tinto – a much bigger foreign mining firm – saw its top Shanghai executive, Stern Hu, locked up in jail in 2010 on controversial grounds.

This chapter will recall Shanghai's treaty-port past and the economic perceptions of the time in order to problematize the imminent rise of the city to global prominence. Touted as Asia's biggest and most cosmopolitan urban centre in the pre-war era, Shanghai has re-emerged since 1991 as a megalopolis dubbed "a harbinger of China's future and a testing ground for the world at large".[5] It is, at the same time, very difficult to judge whether the relative openness on display there is a sign of what is to follow elsewhere in the PRC, or the degree to which this openness betokens overtures toward civil society and more transparent regulatory environment. We shall therefore try to offer a tentative framework for examining these issues.

## History: Records, Literary Allusions

One of many privileges Shanghai historians can nowadays enjoy is staying at the city's oldest-running hotel, the Astor House near Suzhou Creek. It was established as early as 1846 as Richard's Hotel and Restaurant and is known today in Chinese as *Pujiang fandian*. In its heyday, the Astor hosted luminaries like US President Ulysses S. Grant, Charlie Chaplin, Guglielmo Marconi, Albert Einstein, Bernard Russel, journalists Edgar Snow and William Henry Donald and even Zhou Enlai. A 15-minute walk due south, along the ceaselessly re-vamped Bund, is the Shanghai Municipal Archives. There, scholars and historians can relish on demand letters written by the managers of the very same Astor over a century ago, complaining to the foreign-run Shanghai Municipal Council about "natives", "coolies" and "rickshaws" making too much noise for patrons to bear.[6]

Returning to the Astor from the Archives, Shanghai historians can note that road hazards and noise are still a feature of the environment; santanas (a Chinese version of the Volkswagen) have by now supplanted rickshaws as the most common means of transport, and foreigners no longer run the municipal council. Neither is there a sign for Shanghai's once ubiquitous double-deckers and trams, though Soviet-style electric-powered buses still ply the routes between the Bund and Nanjing Rd. from time to time. Historians

might then be reminded that in the 1940s Shanghai's traffic amenities fired up rustic imagination, with newly-imported American
automobiles and regular flights serving the high-heeled between the
city and Hong Kong. The comparable traffic novelty at present is,
of course, the fact that one can, as of 2008, board direct flights from
Pudong International Airport straight to Taipei after years of cross-
strait political chill.[7]

China's relative openness is evident elsewhere too. Official
mouthpieces like the *China Daily* carry occasionally translated op-
ed pieces from, for example, Japan's *Asahi Shinbun*. And against the
backdrop of a global economic crisis, the local press is explicitly
calling for a more transparent central-government stimulus package
to the provinces, warning that such ad hoc funding might be
siphoned off by corrupt officials. The press is otherwise upbeat
about Shanghai's chances of averting a more serious meltdown of
the kind New York and London are now experiencing.[8]

This openness can also be felt in any of Shanghai's countless
bookshops: Gao Xingjian titles are still off limits of course – but a
quieter local variant of Obamania could neverthelss be felt around
the city in 2008, with the First Lady's translated biography selling
fast along side localized editions of anything from *Forbes* to *Marie
Claire*; DVDs of American sitcoms like *Friends*; scores of yoga exercise books; European classics from Dickens to Zola. Even the
flippant-toned Lonely Planet travel guides are on offer in Chinese,
though the LP title to the PRC itself presumably contained too
much politically-sensitive commentary to be approved by censors.
The sheer variety of printed matter is such that one may be tempted
to comb shelves for a Chinese novel of *Slumdog Millionaire* appeal,
only to realize that such searing social critique of the inequalities
attending 'emerging economies' clearly cannot be accommodated
even in this era of PRC openness.

In fact, as Chinese literary scholar Jon von Kowallis recently
noted, Shanghai-born authors have largely shed claims to social
critique, while the PRC publishing industry invariably opts to trans-
late politically-safe foreign titles. The media, more generally, only
broadcasts "ideologically unthreatening" foreign content like
countless dubbed South Korean soap operas – ironically, North
Korean spy thrillers were translated *en masse* in the 1970s because
they were similarly seen in tune with the regime's predilection. For
Kowallis this suggests a Chinese "government alliance with market
forces of the present-day to restrict more and more the translation

of foreign writings, with the exception of Stephen King novels and 'How I Got My Daughter into Harvard with No Sweat' type books."[9]

To be sure, the party-controlled publishing industry is now promoting the collected writings of rehabilitated authors like Ba Jin (aka Li Yaotang, 1904–2005), who had been persecuted as a counter-revolutionary in Shanghai during the Cultural Revolution and lost his wife under these circumstances, but rose in 1983 to become Chairman of the Chinese Writers' Association. At the other end of the spectrum, the book that younger readers perhaps identify with the city the most is strictly banned on the Mainland: Wei Hui's salacious *Shanghai Babe* chronicles a little over a year in the life of CoCo (Ni Ke), a 25-year-old Shanghai novelist. The story revolves around CoCo's emotionally fraught betrayal of her impotent lover Tiantian, her sado-masochistic affair with a married German businessman, and her process of writing a novel that appears to be *Shanghai Babe* itself.

Released in September 1999, the novel had become a best-seller by March 2000 aided in no small part by risqué photographs and comments of Wei Hui in the local media. These led to complaints by Party officials and to state media denunciations of Wei Hui as "decadent, debauched and a slave of foreign culture" and a ban on her novel, which only increased its popularity.[10]

Salacity notwithstanding, Deidre Knight suggested that the novel can perhaps be looked at as bellwether for youth counter-culture in the city and for perceptions of globalization in the non-West. And in this context she finds allusion there to issues like the Shanghainese suspicion of recently-arrived migrant laborers. Yet *Shanghai Babe* evokes sympathy at times for newcomers like hapless door-to-door salesmen and novice taxi drivers who lose their way in the city's interminable motorways; it also bears mention of the suppressed grudge which some local youth feel toward wealthy Western expatriates living in ostentatious closed-quarters, much like in the pre-war era when Chinese entry to some venues was discouraged.[11]

The banning of the book put some potentially acerbic feminist critics of Wei Hui's sensationalism at bay, perhaps because the mainstream literary community did not want to be seen as supporting censorship. When female Shanghai authors Wang Anyi and Wang Zhousheng were asked, for example, about the novel in front of a group of American women artists and scholars, they proclaimed they had not heard of it. Internet chat rooms, on their part, revealed popular disdain for the book's depiction of Chinese masculinity – as epitomized by Tiantian – as impotent compared with Western virility as represented by CoCo's libidinous German lover.[12]

## Economic Take-off: The Triteness of Pudong–Puxi Juxtapositions

Shanghai's cityscape is rapidly transforming itself, while preservation of pre-war architecture is almost inevitably taking the back seat. High-rises are sprawling by leaps and bounds well beyond the pre-war city perimeters.[13] The suburb of Jiangwan, for example, had remained all but a ghost-town on the northern outskirts, even as the KMT was trying to turn it into the city's new civic centre in the late 1930s. The KMT-built Jiangwan stadium, once Asia's largest white elephant, and the eerily empty civic library, are still there – but the suburb itself has since re-invented itself as a hi-tech and tertiary-education powerhouse where Oracle's China headquarters, amongst others, are located.

Similarly, the suburb of Wusong, on the mouth of the Huangpu River, was once regarded as a sparsely-populated (though strategically important) frontier. It is now a crowded mesh of maritime warehouses and shopping malls. The local Qing-era cannon platform (*Wusong paotai*) is the only reminder of the old frontier. The real frontier nowadays is south-western suburbia where "Disney" compounds are being built for the nouveau riche; there is now a huge gated community with perfectly Victorian streets in Songjiang ('Thamestown') and a 'German New Town' near the Volkswagen plant in Anting.

As indicated above, the city's geographical features are quite different to the pre-war setting in both name and substance. Some milestones endured: Nanjing Rd. is still Nanjing Rd.; the once louche Great World Amusement Centre (*Da shijie*) and carefree Wing On (*Yong An*) Department Store are still there, albeit mollified by state ownership; the exquisite *Huxinting* tea house, one of China's oldest, weathers millions of tourists annually. But true to communist frugality, 'Yan'an Rd.' was chosen to replace 'Edward VII Avenue' in what was once the International Settlement. And in what was once the French Settlement, Huaihai Rd. replaced the famously gay 'Avenue Joffre'.

In the 1950s, a Soviet-style Exhibition Centre was built over the semi-legendary Hardoon Garden; streets once named after foreign tycoons like Silas Hardoon or Chinese financier Yu Xiaqing have been 'rectified'. The semi-legendary horserace-course, once lynchpin of white expatriates' social life, has been carved up to make way for the People's Square – Asia's semi-colonial horseracing streak lives on in Hong Kong. China's erstwhile 'Fleet Street', Wangping Rd, is now called Shandong Rd. But the vibrancy of this area which once housed scores of independent publishers is long gone.[14] So too are many of the quaint creeks and canals which had once criss-crossed the city, and were reclaimed in the 1910s to make way for tenements and roads – their traces are barely evident in street names carrying the suffix *bang* or *gang* for 'waterway'. Similarly, the wall which once circled Nantao, or the 'Native City', is only evident in the crescent shape which Renmin Rd. and Zhonghua Rd. form.

Lying west of the Huangpu River, the ultra-modern precinct of Pudong had first been envisioned by Sun Yat-sen, the 'Father of the Nation'. In the 1920s, he pined for a Chinese-run Shanghai that would overshadow what expatriates called 'the model settlement', namely, the International and French concession areas west of the Hunagpu River (Puxi).[15]

Pudong's spectacular skyline has been frantically erected in only two decades, much faster than any other comparable city. If during Sun's time, and through much of the PRC's history, the Bund's waterfront buildings connoted Shanghai's prosperity under European tutelage – today's Pudong vicariously lives up to Sun's vision of overshadowing the old foreign concessions. This symbolism can be scarcely lost on Shanghai historians, and was most certainly on the urban planners' minds in the late 1980s. In fact, Pudong is by now globally unparalleled in many ways: many of its waterfront skyscrapers not only rank among the tallest in the world, but they also light up at night, morphing into gigantic LCD screens. Their glass veneer carry a blend of commercials and local-government *dirigiste* slogans exhorting locals to, for example, congenially greet visitors from other parts of China in standard Mandarin.

It has by now become a trite visitors' observation that Pudong projects Sci-Fi ambience. Multinationals are headquartered there in imposing high-rises, along side even greater edifices housing newly-established semi-state owned corporate entities that are aggressively primed to become the Sony and IBMs of tomorrow. Pudong boasts the world's only magnetic-traction bullet train (Mag-Lav) and a state-of-the-art subway system. Zeppelins screen commercials and slogans overhead as they maneuver their way between skyscrapers.[16]

Yet, as political scientist Justin O'Connor observed, this Sci-Fi ambience does not necessarily augur a budding innovation hub. In his view, "The absence of economic and political pluralism has seriously hampered creativity and innovation within [Shanghai's] knowledge-intensive high-tech and service industries. The West has much higher levels of productivity and innovation; more tellingly, democratic India is overtaking China in terms of software just as other newly democratic countries such as South Korea . . . are producing global brands at a much greater rate than China."[17] And Michel Keane observed in the same volume that " . . . while Shanghai is unquestionably a more cosmopolitan business metropolis", Beijing is the most "multi-cultural city" in China, and a greater magnate for the country's hi-tech and communications industries, as well as for its avant-garde artists and chattering classes.[18]

These observations echo a more profound debate among China watchers as to whether the interventionist development model that typifies Shanghai might reflect a novel, possibly sustainable though chaotic and distinctly Chinese form of 21st-century "capitalism without democracy", as Kellee Tsai alluded to for example; or as renowned economist Huang Yasheng suggests – a deeply-flawed model that stifles individual enterprise and is doomed to failure despite its ability to spawn an awe-inspiring "Potemkin" metropolitan setting such as Pudong.[19]

Moreover, Huang lambasts the local authorities for skewing statistics, and initiating policies that intentionally discriminate against small businesses, and siphoning away income from households in favour of the state-controlled sector, resulting in a flight of innovative start-ups like Alibaba.com to the neighbouring and more *laissez-faire* province of Zhejiang. "Shanghai is rich" but, Huang asserts, " . . . the average Shanghainese is not".[20]

As Jeffrey Wasserstrom noted, the hyperbole surrounding Pudong was set to peak during Expo 2010 with the inauguration of a huge pavilion and bridge complex combining traditional Chinese motifs and the last-word in urban design.[21] Expo 2010 was also supposed to inaugurate the world's first Eco-City, Dongtan, on nearby Chongming Island. Dongtan was designed by the UK-based

Arup Engineering Consortium. However, this particular Expo project has been put on hold for reasons not entirely disclosed. It might ultimately share the fate of the Mag-Lav, another expensive showcase project: for all of its gripping special-effects and dazzling speed, the Mag-Lav fails to reach populous Puxi, and is therefore hardly-used by commuters. Its main proponent, former mayor Chen Liangyu, now languishes in jail on corruption charges.[22]

That said, Pudong for now might seem to the proverbial visitor remarkably unfazed by the global financial crisis: the official line pledges to steam ahead with greater investment in higher-education and R&D (*Kejiao xing shi*). Amid the shine and sparkle, the local English-language media is also reassuring visitors that the global financial crisis is not going to hit Shanghai at all. In 2010, HSBC has moved into its new 250-metre tall China headquarters. Such, analysts were told, is the bank's "confidence . . . in the Chinese economy" that its Pudong home is much taller than its Hong Kong base (180 m) or, for that matter, its London world headquarters (200 m).[23]

There is canny symbolism to all of this. Completed in 1923, the much smaller domed building which rules the Bund skyline on the opposite bank was once HSBC's old China headquarters. That was an era when HSBC was China's *de facto* central bank. In the 1950s, this building was expropriated by the CCP, and in a wry twist of fate, is now home to the state-owned Pudong Development Bank.

In another twist of fate, foreign banks whose forerunners are less associated with colonialism are returning to the Bund waterfront; Citibank and ABN AMRO are but two examples. The former case is particularly interesting since Citibank's other Shanghai building dominates Pudong's skyline from across the river. Citibank accentuates, in that sense, an affiliation with both 'Old' and 'New' Shanghai. But the key question, of course, is whether Citibank's upbeat China outlook can help mitigate its sub-prime crisis at home. Economists are nowadays concerned with the same question posed on larger scale, namely, whether the Chinese economy is starting to 'de-couple' from the ailing US economy on the back of vibrant domestic consumer demand bolstered by fiscal stimuli far greater that the one injected by Western countries.[24]

AIG was a supposedly invincible multinational now groaning under the load of US-derived bad debt – this group and its executive bonuses have provoked alarm in Wall Street and ire on Capitol Hill. However, it seems that only historians are aware that AIG actually owes its rise to prominence to Shanghai in the first place. It was here that Cornelius vander Starr set up the American International Group without much fanfare in 1919. Like HSBC, AIG relocated after the Communist take-over to eventually become – under Hank Greenberg's direction – one of the largest financial arbiters in the world. [25] Like HSBC, it returned to China with a vengeance in the 1990s. But unlike HSBC, which has survived sub-prime vertigo relatively well, AIG's future existence is uncertain. Thus, this is not only a question of Wall Street catching up with Century Avenue, but also of the PRC reminding Wall Street and Capitol Hill of Shanghai's global stature in times past, and of staking out what it sees as the city's rightful claim to the future of global finance.

Whether China's economy is undergoing 'de-coupling' or not, it seems China specialists need to consider the new geo-political alignment more seriously. For years, many were peddling the notion that much of the China boom was oversupply in disguise; that China's implosion was imminent; that at heart this 'economic miracle' was predicated on state-run banks diverting capital to resuscitate moribund state-owned behemoths; that China did not embrace the 'free-market' and 'de-regulate' its economy quickly enough.[26] These attributes might have to do more with Shanghai than with the complex and often uneven economic reform measures in their entirety.

As it turned out in 2008, many leading Western banks do not seem to have allocated capital much more rationally than their PRC counterparts over the last few years.

## 'Shanghaineseness': Identity and Local Media

To try to capture the essence of Shanghainese identity, let alone its permutations over time, would be an inordinately complex task – particularly for an outsider. In order to avoid crude generalizations the following passages will make reference to several authoritative studies, penned by both Shanghainese and foreign scholars, which set out to offer the basic contours of this identity.

The Shanghainese cannot be easily tarred with the same brush. This is not least because the city has re-emerged as a magnate for a motley crew of new residents ranging from micro-entrepreneurs to fresh university graduates, young artists and menial labourers from all over China. It is also attracting more and more western expatriates of all socio-economic rungs, though their ratio of the city's population is still smaller than in the 1930s.

Nevertheless, as Marie-Claire Bergere and Jos Gamble have observed in their respective studies, the locally-born population is very different in its social makeup from the enterprising Ningbo sojourners who formed the elite of 'Old Shanghai' in the 1850s. Ironically, the strict *hukou* residency restrictions of Mao's era engendered a linguistically and culturally cohesive sense of Shanghaineseness. Notably, the city was quite subdued during the 1989 student protest movement, and since 1991 has been smothered in preferential central-government funding.[27]

Established Shanghainese households of today are often described as a born-and-bred privileged corps; they come across as "aloof" and suspicious of outsiders in James Farrer's recently-published anthropological study.[28] On the whole, they are described as much more inward-looking and risk-averse than their migrant-society forebears: those resourceful sojourners who had converged on the city from every corner of China at the turn of the 20th century. Moreover, Shanghainese men are often stereotyped as timid, calculating and effeminate in popular culture.

Interestingly, eminent Shanghai historian Xiong Yuezhi (b. 1949, Jiangsu province) seems to agree that many locals possess a "sense of superiority", which he attributes to the city's pre-war association with all things Western, and to the fact that, even when its economy was emaciating in the 1950s, the city still contributed at least a quarter of central-government tax revenue. But he also suggests that, despite their predilection for Shanghainese dialect or Putonghua, many locals are still conscious of their ancestral migrant roots in Fujian, Guangdong or Zhejiang.[29]

The 1950s–70s legacy of heavy-handed indoctrination under hardline mayor Ke Qingshi, the Red Guards, Shanghai Commune and the Gang of Four have all entrenched Shanghai in the popular mindset as a bastion of CCP conservatism perhaps irrevocably. Mao famously pitted Shanghai's media against Beijing cadres when launching the Anti-Rightist Campaign of the late 1950s and later the Cultural Revolution. After Mao's death, Shanghai's media was commandeered equally forcefully to trumpet Deng's reform, to the

extent that today while being one of China's richest and most adver-
tisement-saturated cities – the local media is arguably China's
"tamest" and most "risk averse".[30]

By and large, the city's art scene and media are still more strictly
monitored than in Beijing. Art activities in the city are overseen by
the Shanghai Cultural Bureau, which still imposes repressive
censorship even by Chinese standards. For example, until recently,
official permits were rarely granted for rock concerts; a de facto ban
on covering alternative music seems to be in effect in the local
media; the Bureau of Broadcasting, Film, and Television monitors
all documentaries and other film related activities; the Cultural
Bureau inspects all major theatre play rehearsals.[31] It thus should
come as no surprise that Beijing is preferred by many artists and
entrepreneurs who resile from state co-optation, and that
Guangzhou's media is widely seen as the most outspoken in China
with its daring coverage of, for example, the spread of SARS (severe
acute respiratory syndrome) and the authorities' incompetence in
dealing with it.[32]

In recent years, television content has once again greatly diversified after a temporary recoil in the wake of the Tiananmen Square
Riots (1989). Despite the entry into the Chinese markets of foreign-
owned Chinese-language providers like HBO, Phoenix TV, MTV,
Discovery and others, diversification is heavily geared toward light-
entertainment and finance news. There are over 30 foreign satellite
channels that have been allowed restricted transmission rights in
Shanghai – most are entertainment-focused. When it comes to
politically sensitive news items, they exercise what Ruoyun Bai has
called "market censorship": private media have developed a self-
censorship mechanism minutely-attuned to national policy
imperatives so as not to lose their licence. Interestingly, even
confined as it is to entertainment, provincial satellite channels like
that of Hunan, which are peripheral and therefore less strictly regulated, often post higher ratings than local competitors like Dragon
TV (Dongfang weishi).[33]

Nevertheless, other local media – particularly radio – seem to play
a pivotal role in re-imagining what Mayfair Yang called "transnational subjectivity", that is the provisioning of narratives that elide
the doctrinaire. They help cement a new urban identity that is
permeated with Hong Kong and Taiwanese popular culture. The
latter temper the significance of Western content, and eclipse
Hollywood's socio-political significance as trend-setter. Yang simi-

larly points to the Shanghai-based Oriental Broadcasting Co. (*Dongfang guangbo diantai*, est. 1993) as antidote to the radio transmissions from Beijing during the height of the Cultural Revolution. In the Maoist era proletarian model operas (*yangbanxi*) and Mandarin voices "over-coded" the CCP's nation-building project. Today by contrast the Oriental Broadcasting Co. regularly features traditional *tanci* sketches performed in *Shanghainese*, and airs call-ins from listeners, who often lapse into localisms.[34]

This overview collated a wide range of anecdotal evidence from contemporary Shanghai in a bid to sketch out how its historic self-perception, changing economic makeup and local media have changed over three decades of reform. Particular emphasis was placed on Shanghai's architectural makeover, and the ways in which it is invoking the boom-times of the 1930s to conjure up newly-found cosmopolitanism. Nevertheless, the city looks remarkably different than in the 1930s, and pockets of intact pre-war tenements are increasingly hard to find. Precarious as it is, the invocation of the past is mobilized to legitimize and revalidate the city's unbridled consumerism nowadays.

Pudong has come to symbolize Shanghai's rebirth, but many see it as a cup half-empty: far from suggesting dynamism and innovation it is widely seen as testament to wasteful diversion of tax-payers' money that ultimately translates into impoverished local households as compared with the state-controlled sector; at worst, it is described as a Potemkin megalopolis that masks a miasmic urban society, dormant media and a literary scene that is risk-averse.

There is fairly broad agreement amongst historians and analysts of contemporary China that Shanghai of the 1930s was truly remarkable in its degree of relative openness and cosmopolitanism – notwithstanding the rife racialism of that era. Though some commentators would even suggest that the pre-war era might be worthy of invoking at present – there is disagreement as to whether the city's current growth model builds on that pre-war experience. At the one extreme, critics like Huang Yasheng predict that CCP measures preferential to Shanghai will inevitably reach a dead-end, and eventually give way to policy fostering rural entrepreneurship and small business instead. Fleeting visitors, on the other hand, continue to marvel at the "miracle" unfolding in Pudong perhaps because simplistic juxtapositions such as that of Pudong–Puxi can only hold up on a short-term basis.

Many observers point to the permutation of Shanghainese identity itself. Locals take pride in the city's pre-war history and its reputation for receptivity to the West. But, as tracts of Wei Hui's novel and the reactions it elicited suggest, there may still be some repressed grudge against wealthy foreigners – the spectre of imperialism and "national humiliation" can be potentially fanned and manipulated by the party-state to deflect domestic criticism. That grudge came to the boil again in 2012 as many in Shanghai took to the streets to protest against Japan's nationalization of the Senkaku Islets, known to the Chinese as Diaoyu Islets. The protests entailed a strident popular boycott of Japanese brands reminiscent of the pre-war era.

However, suspicion of foreigners has a flipside: it is often directed at outsiders broadly defined (e.g. Chinese rural migrant workers seeking employment in the city). Ironically, stereotypes of the Shanghainese as dismissive of outsiders, aloof, effeminate and risk-averse or as fawning Westerners and Japanese are quite common in the PRC popular discourse.

In the face of such discourse, this chapter has pointed to the greater access that is now granted to the city's archival records; to the ubiquity of foreign-media content, both printed and electronic; to the rehabilitation and promotion of once 'subversive' literature such as that penned by Ba Jin; and to what may be an epoch-making move to allow the flotation of foreign-firm stock on the local stock exchange.

This anecdotal evidence is often understated, but should nonetheless be seriously considered if academics are to have a nuanced view of the PRC. Engaging the PRC with an *open*-mind is called for even if, on balance, the evidence falls short of bearing out the case for a completely open China.

## Notes

1 The Shanghai Municipal Archives online catalogue is available at: http://www.archives.sh.cn:9080/newcatalog2/newmenu/newmenu.jsp ?do=js [Accessed 10 November 2013]; on the Zikawei library collection – see http://travel.nytimes.com/travel/guides/asia/china/ shanghai/ attraction-detail.html?vid=1154654615873 [Accessed 10 November 2013].

2 Portraying the transition to communism in early 1950s Shanghai as

one of gradualness, Swislocki (2009) suggests austerity measures were not implemented uniformly in the city. He then brilliantly marshals recently-declassified material from the SMA, which shows for example that up until the Cultural Revolution (i.e. between 1949 and1966) the municipal Communist Party apparatus had cultivated chefs with exceptional talents and a flair for food as exotic as 'elephant trunk' (p. 215).

3 On the popularity and availability of foreign satellite television in Iran, see e.g. Barraclough (2001).

4 See http://en.ce.cn/Business/Enterprise/200905/12/t20090512_19051631.shtml [Accessed 10 November 2013].

5 See Rowe and Kuan (2004), p. 6.

6 For later correspondence between Astor managers and the Shanghai Municipal Council see, e.g., SMA File no. U1-3-467 from 1924.

7 See http://www.reuters.com/article/pressRelease/idUS66328+25-Jun-2008+PRN20080625 [Accessed 10 November 2013].

8 On corruption, see e.g. http://www.chinadaily.com.cn/china/2009-02/20/content_7494648.htm [Accessed 10 November 2013]; for GFC pep talk, see e.g. http://www.chinadaily.com.cn/china/2009-02/20/content_7494674.htm [Accessed 10 November 2013].

9 Kowallis (2009).

10 On the *Shanghai Babe* literary phenomenon, see Knight (2003); Weber (2002).

11 Knight (2003), p. 644.

12 Zhong (2006), pp. 647–648.

13 On architectural preservation in Shanghai and the fast-changing cityscape, see Zhang (2005); Rowe and Kuan (2004).

14 On Wangping Rd. see e.g. Reed (2004), pp. 181, 289.

15 On Sun Yat-sen's vision of Pudong, see Henriot (1993).

16 On the triteness of Pudong's designation as futuristic, see Wasserstrom (2009).

17 O'Connor (2009), p. 177.

18 Keane (2009), p. 82. See also Wu (2004), cited below; Huang (2008, pp. 193–194) observed that Beijing, not Shanghai, dominates the list of the technological start-ups that have gone public on NASDAQ. Similarly, he notes that since 1990 there has been a stark drop in Shanghai's share of national patent registration.

19 Tsai (2009); Huang (2008).

20 Huang (2008), p. 183.

21 Wasserstrom (2009).

22 On Chen Liangyu, see Zheng (2006).

23 See http://www.hsbc.com/1/2/newsroom/news/news-archive-2007/hsbc-china-headquarters-to-move-to-new-building-in-shanghai-ifc-shkp-s-new-pudong-landmark [Accessed 10 November 2013].

24  See http://ipsnews.net/news.asp?idnews=40903 [Accessed 10 November 2013].

25  Shelp (2006).

26  See e.g. Chang (2001).

27  Gamble (2003), pp. 86–90.

28  Farrer (2008).

29  Xiong (1996).

30  Lee et al. (2007).

31  Wu (2004).

32  Esarey (2005).

33  Bai (2005).

34  Yang (2002).

# 6

## Epilogue

## No Longer in the Shadow of Hong Kong

### The History of Hong Kong's Economic Development

Having undergone three successful economic reconfigurations since its founding as a British colony in 1841, by the 1980s Hong Kong had consolidated its position as a leading international centre of trade, finance, and shipping. The three main phases were the colony's transformation from what many Britons considered to be a 'barren rock' into an important entrepôt and the beacon of British administrative, military, and educational presence in East Asia; Hong Kong's absorption of Mainland industrial and entrepreneurial skills in the 1950s, which transformed it into a textile powerhouse; and its metamorphosis into the second most important harbour and equity-market venue in East Asia in the late 1970s.[1]

After its handover to the People's Republic of China (PRC) in 1997, and in the face of the Asian Financial Crisis, the government of Hong Kong SAR set in train a number of reforms designed to achieve early recovery. In particular, great efforts were made toward fostering the tertiary sector and seeding new high-tech industries. Although this most recent phase of economic reconfiguration has proven less successful than the previous two, Hong Kong has come to play a critical role as the gateway to the Mainland economy's globalization.[2]

Following the Second Opium War (1856–1860), Britain took control of the southern part of the Kowloon Peninsula and the waters between Hong Kong Island and the Peninsula. These 'new territories' became an important platform for the rapid development of Hong Kong's entrepôt trade. As the Industrial Revolution spread from England to other Western countries in the latter part of the 19th century, the West's industrial output increased, generating an urge to find new markets overseas. The importance of Hong Kong thus loomed larger, as many in the West entertained ambitions of enrichment by way of penetration of the vast Chinese hinterland via Hong Kong. From 1867 to 1900 the percentage of goods trans-shipped via Hong Kong of the total imported by China rose from 20 per cent to 40 per cent.[3]

It was the Korean War in the 1950s that helped transform Hong Kong's entrepôt, trade-driven economic structure into a textile powerhouse. The US had placed an economic blockade on communist China; under US pressure, Britain followed. As Mainland China's largest transit point, Hong Kong experienced a sharp reduction in the volume of trade and was forced to look for other markets. Given the war-time hindrances and the suspension of traffic to and from the Mainland, Hong Kong businesses had no alternative in the pursuit of profit and economic recovery but to develop their own industries. Outside influences aside, the fact that Hong Kong had accumulated a large capital base in the pre-war era also contributed to rapid industrialization. This accumulation of capital partly originated in the Kuomintang (KMT) government's diversion to Hong Kong of funds just before it surrendered the Mainland to the CCP; as well as from the flight of wealthy or educated refugees from the Mainland who feared communist reprisal, and who enhanced the colony's human capital and technical knowledge base.[4]

In the 1980s China's 'open-door' policy affected Hong Kong's economic development. Since China wooed foreign investment in manufacturing by highlighting its cheap-labour edge, many Hong Kong firms quickly moved their own labour-intensive industries to the Pearl River Delta. In turn, the colony was to focus – from then until its handover – on fostering its finance and shipping sectors. This third economic restructuring proved a great success, as the percentage of manufacturing output relative to total output continued to decline. Tertiary industry replaced secondary industry to become Hong Kong's largest employer by the 1980s; and by 1997 tertiary industry absorbed 72.5 per cent of Hong Kong's workforce.[5]

In his analysis of the history and provenance of Hong Kong's third economic restructuring, Chen Guanghan (2009) suggests that another important catalyst for this change was the competitive pressure placed on Hong Kong's manufacturing industry by the export-led economies of neigbouring countries such as South Korea, Singapore, and Thailand, as well as resurgent trade protectionism in the international market. Against this backdrop, and in the light of its government's *laissez-faire* guiding principles, resource-scarce Hong Kong was forced to lift efficiency in services and higher added-value industries so as to raise its level of export competitiveness.[6]

When the 1997 Asian economic crisis began and property and stock markets plunged, the Hong Kong economy entered a period of temporary decline. Hong Kong was still struggling to stem the decline even as the situation in the other four Asian tigers steadily improved. This brought to light problems at the heart of the Hong Kong economy. In contrast to Singapore where the high-tech sector was nestled within a more diversified industrial structure, the Hong Kong economy lacked clear industrial guidance, with the result that the city gradually lost much of its secondary industry. This loss is the motivating factor behind the government's more pro-active sponsorship of the current phase of redevelopment, which aims to create a stronger high-tech sector and a more diversified services sector.

Yet, despite deeper government involvement, the third redevelopment phase has not been as successful as the previous phases; in part because of the long-term adverse effect on business confidence of the SARS epidemic and, more recently, because demand for new high-tech outsourcing services is still subdued in the US and the Eurozone following the Global Financial Crisis. In addition, the flight of labour-intensive industries to the Pearl River Delta has meant higher rates of unemployment of unskilled workers in Hong Kong; workers were not adequately re-trained to join the nascent high-tech industries, thus forcing the city to rely on imported expertise to sustain its foray into that area. Notably, Hong Kong-listed firms employ many more workers (and not just blue-collar ones) in the Pearl River Delta and Southeast Asia than in the former colony itself.[7]

## Shanghai's Trajectory in Comparison

The economic development of Shanghai followed a different path from that of Hong Kong but, like the former colony, it was by no means linear. As recounted in previous chapters, from its designation in 1843 as a treaty-port, Shanghai quickly became the world's gateway to the Yangtze Delta, and could boast a solid industrial base and global reputation by the 1920s.[8] Shanghai's preeminence was partly due to its proximity to China's relatively affluent silk- and tea-producing areas, where British-conveyed opium could easily be distributed. In 1852, Shanghai replaced Guangzhou as China's largest international port – a further step in shoring up its position as the Mainland's most important commercial hub. From 1846 to 1853 the share of Chinese tea exported via Shanghai grew from 14 per cent to approximately 70 per cent.[9]

Trade income combined with consumer demand turned Shanghai into an all-important cultural and industrial hub.[10] Prior to 1890, the foreign exchange market in Shanghai was exclusively in the hands of the British; but the ensuing rivalry between British, French, German, Belgian, and American consortia greatly diversified and expanded the city's financial markets – even when they presented a united front to keep up favourable loan repayment conditions forced on the Qing dynasty. This competition, coupled with the rise of modern banking centred in the city, brought about a boom in industrial development and financial market growth that greatly exceeded that of Hong Kong under stricter British rule.[11]

After the communist take-over in 1949, the central government in Beijing assumed absolute power over Shanghai's economic, political, and cultural spheres. But the transition to a planned economy was fairly cautious. Since the West imposed a trade embargo on the newly-established PRC, Shanghai's role changed from one driven by global trade and a vibrant urban consumer culture to one defined by Chairman Mao's early attempt at self-reliance and promoting the relocation of industry further inland.[12]

Central planning and the focus on the inland constrained the pace of economic development in Shanghai. From its origins as a centre of commerce, the city was transformed into a manufacturing plant for the entire country. In 1952 secondary industry accounted for 52.4 per cent of Shanghai's Gross Product and tertiary industry for 41.7 per cent; but by 1978 the share of secondary industry had risen to 77.4 per cent.[13] Shanghai had, without interruption, continued to contribute goods and capital. In 1978, Shanghai's fiscal expenditures comprised a mere 14.6 per cent of local fiscal revenue – the lion's share of its revenue was reallocated elsewhere by the central government.[14]

The Chinese Communist Party's (CCP) Central Committee embarked on the open-door policy (*gaige kaifang*) at the Third Plenary Session of the 11th Communist Party of China Central Committee in 1978; but during the ensuing period of national economic recovery, Shanghai was not in the advance guard of the new era. Until 1991, the pace of its development lagged behind that of Guangdong, Shandong, and other provinces; not to mention other cities in the Yangtze River Delta. In the years between 1978 and 1990, the average growth of Shanghai's GDP was 8.9 per cent – well below the national average of 14.7 per cent. [15]

The reason for this lower growth lies in the central government's adherence to the principle of minimising social instability. By isolating Shanghai from reform measures, in effect the central government indemnified itself against unexpected loss of fiscal revenue, and eschewed being seen as reviving the city's pre-war liberal economic legacy. [16] It was feared that local government departments and the workforce at large would mount organized resistance to any withdrawal of the benefits, entitlements, job security, and productive mindset of the era of central planning. In 1978, as the reforms pressed ahead in other coastal cities, state-owned enterprises comprised 42.4 per cent of Shanghai's industrial and commercial businesses and state-owned enterprises accounted together for 91.7 per cent of the city's total output value – a much higher proportion than the national average of 77.6 per cent. [17]

Deng Xiaoping's eagerness to speed up reforms in the face of international condemnation of the Tiananmen Square massacre of 1989 drew national attention back to Shanghai. In 1992, Deng, on the basis of a thorough knowledge of the theoretical and practical experience of the 1980s, gave his affirmation of, and support to, the opening up of the Pudong Special Development Area. At the time, Pudong was an underdeveloped precinct of Shanghai, lying east of the Huangpu river, along which the city's historic CBD was strung. At the 14th CCP Congress held in October that year, Pudong was officially designated as the future economic heartland of the Lower Yangtze Delta. From this point on, Shanghai stood at the forefront of the economic reform policy, with the strategic aim of turning the city into China's centre of finance, trade, and shipping by 2020. Shanghai's GDP growth not only exceeded the national average thereafter but also re-assumed some of its pre-war stature as a global cultural hub. [18]

Yet, despite Shanghai's faster pace of development between

1992 and 2012 as compared to Hong Kong, it is still widely seen as less global and entrepreneurial. If anything, Hong Kong's position as a financial centre has strengthened in recent years, and it is now ranked number one in the world in that regard by the World Economic Forum.[19] Neither is the opening of Shanghai's Disneyland in 2015 seen as a threat to Hong Kong's tourist industry.[20] The following sections underscore the remaining commonalities and differences between the economies of Shanghai and Hong Kong.

## Competition or Complements?

On 29 June 2003, Commerce Department Deputy Minister An Min, representing the central government in Beijing, signed, along with the Hong Kong SAR Financial Secretary Leung Kam Chung, the *Mainland and Hong Kong Closer Economic Partnership Arrangement* (CEPA). Six supplementary agreements have been concluded in the years since, resulting in smoother cross-border traffic and further integrating the former colony into the Mainland's emerging economy.[21]

The CEPA and supplementary agreements designated such products as electrical machinery, paper products, and cosmetics as tariff-free. These agreements have broadened the terms of entry by Hong Kong service-sector companies into Mainland markets. It will now be easier for Hong Kong-based travel agencies, banks, securities, law firms, and logistics to set up a more robust presence anywhere in China. The heart of economic and trade cooperation between the two cities no longer lies in trade in manufactured goods but rather in high-end services – with an annual rate of growth of approximately 20 per cent since 2004. The number of PRC nationals visiting Hong Kong each year subsequently rose from 15.5 million to 29.6 million from 2003 to 2009. Concomitantly, from 1993 to 2009 Shanghai's trade volume with Hong Kong grew at 21.6 per cent.[22]

The beneficial macro-economic environment in which linkages between the two cities have been enhanced owes much to the PRC government's experiments with RMB internationalization via Hong Kong. At the end of 2008, the Shanghai Delta region and Hong Kong conducted a pilot on the use of the renminbi in trade settlement. At the beginning of 2009, another pilot was conducted on cross-border trade settlement with the administrative centre based in Hong Kong. Cooperation between the Shanghai and Hong Kong banking sectors was necessary to construct a global system for the cross-border use of the currency in order to ensure the smooth circulation of funds and the supply of renminbi in clearance and settlement mechanisms, both domestically and internationally.[23]

In 2007, the first issue of renminbi-denominated bonds was floated in Hong Kong by the PRC government; in more recent times, both foreign and Mainland enterprises have been allowed to mobilise funds through renminbi-denominated corporate securities offered for sale exclusively in Hong Kong. The Hong Kong Monetary Authority, the People's Bank of China, the China Insurance Regulatory Commission, and the China Banking Regulatory Commission stepped up cooperation at this point to eliminate barriers to trade in renminbi-denominated assets between the Mainland and the former colony.[24]

Aside from cooperation in the economic sphere, people-to-people and educational ties between Shanghai and Hong Kong have also expanded. Shanghai's high school graduates increasingly look to attend Hong Kong universities as a substitute to expensive degrees from western universities.[25] Many local businesses offer work-exchange opportunities in Shanghai and Hong Kong to their employees. Interaction among technicians, academics, and finance and law professionals is frequent, facilitating the transfer of know-how in both directions.

## Natural Endowments, Production Factors, and Global Prestige

Shanghai and Hong Kong both benefit from comparatively advantageous locations. Situated on the southern shore of the mouth of the Yangtze River, Shanghai is within easy reach of the Yangtze Delta hinterland and in close proximity to industrial cities such as Nanjing, Hangzhou, Ningbo, Wuxi, and Changzhou. Hong Kong is perched on the South China Sea and straddles the Pearl River Delta. Both cities straddle busy shipping lanes in the Asia-Pacific region. In 2007, Shanghai's new container port became the second largest in the world in terms of capacity, and today (2014) is the world's largest by a wide margin. Honk Kong's port, having been the largest in Asia for many years, is still the third largest in the world in terms of capacity, and the second largest servicing the Mainland.[26]

Hong Kong has been able to leverage its position as a Special Administrative Region (SAR) under the 'one Country, two systems' policy to bolster its attractiveness to foreign investors who seek greater access to the Chinese market but are wary of the vagaries of Chinese corporate law. The former colony retains its autonomy and may participate independently in international conferences; it also has autonomous decision-making authority on issues of local development. By contrast, as Shanghai is under the direct supervision of the central government, its power to enact its own policies is more constricted.[27]

However, in recent years, central government policy has encouraged Shanghai to re-brand itself as an open cosmopolitan hub. Spectacles such as the 2010 World Expo and a variety of sporting and cultural events have pitted Shanghai against Hong Kong.[28] Yet, to a large extent, Hong Kong retains the aura of 'small government, big market', based on a simpler taxation system, a more transparent regulatory environment, and a relatively efficient public sector that typified much of the colonial era.[29] Aside from replicating these conditions, how to establish the integrity of the market system, how to recruit and train human resources, and how to create a stable social environment, are lessons that Shanghai would do well to learn from Hong Kong's experience with development.[30]

## The Impact of the Global Financial Crisis

The 2008 Global Financial Crisis (GFC) proved a temporary blow to the two cities' economies; however, their responses to the crisis were very different. The growth of Shanghai's GDP fell in 2008 and 2009 because its export-oriented manufacturing industry makes it particularly susceptible to global demand slumps. Under these circumstances, Shanghai has set itself the goal of diversifying its markets and stimulating consumer demand.[31]

But apart from its negative impact, the financial crisis opened up opportunities for Shanghai. In fact, following the financial crisis, the US stepped up regulation of newly-created financial instruments such as hedge and private equity funds. This move prompted several US funds to relocate their headquarters overseas. Given the fast development of the finance industry and the vigorous demand for finance capital, Shanghai, as the Mainland's financial centre, provided an excellent platform for the entry of the US financial industry.[32]

By comparison, Hong Kong's economy was worse hit by the GFC, although it has strongly rebounded over the past two years with 7 per cent annual growth.[33] The global standing of Hong Kong's financial industry has also improved since 2008. Quite apart from Hong Kong's designation as a launch pad for the renmbi internationalization strategy, the proportion of IPOs floated in the Hong Kong securities market in 2009 comprised 22 per cent of the world total, with the great bulk representing Mainland corporate equity (H-shares). Moreover, increasing numbers of Mainland enterprises have chosen to invest in Hong Kong as their first overseas destination. [34]

In May 2001, the State Council issued an *Approval of the Shanghai Urban Master Plan*, which affirmed the city as an all-important economic centre. The *Approval* notes that sustainable development is the key objective with a focus on the financial and insurance sectors, as well as innovative information technology; to improve city services in order to build a 'prosperous, socially enlightened and environmentally pleasant international metropolis'.[35]

Beginning in the 1990s, in order to promote its finance industry the Hong Kong government introduced a series of supportive measures. It reduced several restrictions on the establishment of foreign bank branches. Next, the government revoked the upper limit of seven days or less on time deposit and savings deposit rates In addition, Hong Kong established the Real Time Gross Settlement Systems (RTGS), which make it much easier for investors to settle accounts interchangeably in HK$, US$, RMB, or Euro. A bilateral network of debt instruments, the Central Money Markets Unit (CMU), was also put in place whereby international central securities depositories can transact funds more seamlessly.[36]

Hong Kong's share of the GDP of the Greater Pearl River Delta is large; its per capita GDP is greater than that of Shanghai and, indeed, is greater than that of any other city in the Greater Pearl River Delta region. Large-scale financial institutions and multinational enterprises (MNEs) are mostly headquartered in Hong Kong.

Whether a region can host a concentration of MNE headquarters depends on the extent to which it is able to maintain international standards, particularly with respect to intellectual property rights. In this respect, Hong Kong maintains superiority over Shanghai. At the end of 2009, Hong Kong was host to the regional headquarters of 1,298 MNEs, whereas for Shanghai the number was only 260. In addition, Hong Kong has a concentration of a larger number of widely-recognized insurance, banking, and mutual funds enterprises.[37]

Hong Kong's competence in financial regulation lays the groundwork for the development of a more sustainable service industry. The city's tax system is comparatively simple, with a flat corporate tax rate of a mere 24.4 per cent. Moreover, Hong Kong does not impose additional business duties and is therefore ranked as one of most business-friendly places in the world. By comparison, Shanghai's domestic corporate tax burden can reach as high as 73.9 per cent, second only to Beijing's. Hong Kong's low tax rate has proven a compelling draw-card for foreign investment and expatriate expertise.[38]

Financial market have always possessed a high level of internationalization in the former colony. Since 2005, these markets have also gradually become a high-quality financial platform for Mainland enterprises. Furthermore, the proliferation of types of financial products has been completely opened up to international investors including stocks, bonds, funds, options futures, and the gold market. Hong Kong has promulgated several ordinances with the aim of enacting a system of inspection – establishing reasonable rules of market risk assessment, transparency, and efficiency.[39] Yet, repercussions from global events affect Hong Kong's capital markets more than they do Shanghai's or Shenzhen's. During the US financial crisis, Hong Kong's total stock market capitalization was more than halved: falling from HK$20.5 trillion to just HK$10.2 trillion.[40]

The scope for development in Shanghai's economic hinterland is far greater than that of the Pearl and Yangtze River Delta, which is already industrialized. The location of many of China's largest 500 enterprises is in the Jiangsu–Zhejiang region. The potential for transformative IPOs seems greater in Shanghai as many of the said companies have not fully listed yet.[41]

The Shanghai Stock Exchange's total market capitalization has now exceeded that of Hong Kong and is now Asia's second largest, although trade volumes remain lower as much of the corporate stock is immobilized under state ownership. Yet, compared to Hong Kong, direct capital mobilization by privately-managed corporations in Shanghai is inadequate; the volume of equity transactions makes up only one-quarter of the transactions mediated through bank credit. In Hong Kong, on the other hand, the ratio has stabilized at around two-thirds. Equity transaction costs in Shanghai are also higher due to the greater reliance on bank intermediation.[42]

Studies by Morck, Yeung and Yu (2000) and Chen Zhiwu (2006) posit that in evaluating the market efficiency of China's securities market one must bear in mind that between 1991 and 2005 correlation between individual stock prices was more than 80 per cent – a far higher rate than the 57 per cent of US securities markets. In other words, individual Chinese-listed stock prices are swayed to a larger degree by market sentiment than by factors such as individual company profits – a key indicator of lack of confidence on the part of investors in the veracity of the data published by companies on their growth potential and earnings.[43]

Remarkably, from 2000 to 2004 Hong Kong stock prices were a more accurate predictor of the growth rate of China's GDP than the Shanghai Composite Index for the same period. Several years later, the capital markets of Shanghai and Hong Kong were both greatly affected by the global upswing in share prices in 2007 as well as the crash of 2008. Both the Shanghai Composite Index and the total market capitalization of H-shares severely deviated from the real economy; this fact, whether in Hong Kong or in Shanghai, points to the appearance of a serious bubble in their capital markets before the financial crisis.[44]

Because Shanghai is not yet able to match the global cachet, low corporate tax rate, family-friendly lifestyle, and amenities that Hong Kong offers, senior expatriate professionals still tend to prefer Hong Kong as their base in Greater China. At the same time, a massive outflow of talent from Shanghai to foreign countries has occurred. Thus, the core of Shanghai's finance professionals hails primarily from China and lacks international exposure.[45] The number of financial institutions in Shanghai has been lower than in Hong Kong and Singapore; and its product range is more limited to traditional investments such as stocks and bonds. This situation is further encumbered by government regulation that imposes barriers between Chinese and foreign investors through separate stock listings.[46]

## Social Inequalities

Economic growth and social stability will always be two of the key problems national or local government must confront in China. Factors affecting social stability include the gap between rich and poor, the rate of unemployment, education and health status, and welfare entitlements. From the 1990s, Hong Kong's Gini coefficient has been at 0.5 or above. In 2006, the Hong Kong Census and Statistics Department announced that the Gini coefficient had reached 0.53, higher than other developed regions.[47]

The Gini coefficient is lowest in Europe, where for many countries it is less than 0.4. Among the developing countries, Asia-Pacific countries have a comparatively low coefficient; whereas among Asian nations and regions, Hong Kong's Gini coefficient has been consistently high. In comparison to Hong Kong, Mainland China's Gini coefficient stood at 0.15 in the early 1980s; however, the increase in income disparity and economic growth went hand-in-hand. Up to 2007, the Gini coefficient for China's cities was only 0.42. Later, despite an absence of authoritative statistical data, a panoply of problems brought on by the rich–poor divide has continually come to the fore.[48]

Imbalances in the distribution of income have become progressively more acute; wealth and power have become concentrated in the hands of a few well-connected tycoons.[49] Since such aspects of a social welfare system as social security, universal medical care, and education have yet to meet Western European levels, and since the gap between ordinary people's standard of living and that of the rich and powerful and well-connected has widened, a minority of Hong Kong residents, who consider themselves particularly disenfranchised, contend that they do not partake of the former colony's global stature.[50]

On the other hand, Hong Kong joined the ranks of developed regions comparatively early and its social structure is mature compared to Shanghai. Although its Gini coefficient continues to be higher than in countries in the developed world, many social problems that have emerged in Mainland China did not come to the boil in Hong Kong. An important reason for this is that – in response to pro-Mao local demonstrations by the disenfranchised in the late 1960s – Hong Kong had already successfully created a social atmosphere of fair competition and transparency and an entrepreneurial ethos alongside the selective provisioning of public housing for the poor, particularly during Murray MacLehose's tenure as Governor (1972–1981).

Though rugged individualism and risk-prone entrepreneurialism are on the wane, Hong Kong society still advocates the concept of 'no pain, no gain', and for this reason popular resentment of successful entrepreneurs is quite rare. Moreover, through an effective mitigating redistribution program, Hong Kong has secured all its residents' elementary needs as regards medical care, health, education, and public amenities; though this program is targeted in orientation, and falls far short of Scandinavian standards, it is quite extensive by Asian standards. In addition, a relatively well-developed insurance industry has not only enhanced ordinary people's sense of security but may have also contributed to the relatively high levels of personal contentment reported in occasional surveys.[51]

## Conclusions and Future Prospects for Growth

Shanghai and Hong Kong have, under different economic conditions, followed dissimilar but equally difficult paths of development; but both have won the world's recognition. Despite the Global Financial Crisis, Shanghai was nevertheless still able to achieve an 8.2 per cent GDP growth rate. Although Hong Kong experienced negative growth during the crisis, it has seen a slow recovery by 2010.

It is undeniable that Shanghai's development momentum is higher than Hong Kong's owing to its different foundations of growth and different starting point. Yet, overall, it is difficult to envision Shanghai overtaking Hong Kong in the near future. While it is a more important shipping hub nowadays, Shanghai is unlikely to dethrone Hong Kong as a regional financial hub in the near future, particularly in view of the dominant position assigned to the latter by the PRC government insofar as facilitating the renminbi's internationalization. Neither will the inauguration of the Shanghai Free Trade Zone in 2013 necessarily tarnish Hong Kong's uniqueness, as the extent of media openness, tax rates and currency convertibility in the Zone are not yet entirely clear to investors. At their present stages of development, it will be important for each of these two cities to identify and enhance their respective strengths and gain insights from each other's evolution.

Partly driven by initiatives such as CEPA, linkages between

Shanghai and Hong Kong will expand in the future; such linkages may well assist these two powerhouses of China's coastal region in leading the drive toward opening up China's western provinces for investment, thereby mitigating regional disparities across the Mainland. Learning from Hong Kong's experience may assist Shanghai in diversifying its services sector and in improving its capacity for innovation and global reach. In that sense, Hong Kong may become a midwife to Shanghai's further internationalization. By the same token, the quality of scientific research conducted in Shanghai, its human capital, and industrial base, as well as its potential market demand, will continue to drive Hong Kong's economic recovery and third phase of economic restructuring. Where both cities will need to do better in order to become more viable economically is in fostering high-tech industries that can offset their reliance on shipping and finance.

## Notes

1 For recent authoritative overviews of Hong Kong's economic history under British rule, see, e.g. Faure (2003), Faure and Lee (2004), Tsang (2007), Carroll (2007), and Schenk (2007).
2 N'Diaye and Ahuja (2012).
3 See Liu (1997).
4 Wong (1988).
5 China National Bureau of Statistics (1999).
6 Chen (2009), pp. 78–9.
7 Baark and So (2006), Lui and Chiu (2009), pp. 93–124.
8 Murphey (1986), pp. 79–80.
9 Shanghai Economists' Association (1992).
10 Xiong (1999), pp. 15–21.
11 Yao (1990), pp. 19–20; Cheng (2003).
12 During the period of Soviet technical assistance to China inaugurated by the first Five-Year Plan (1953–1957) not a single project was slated for Shanghai in the overall distribution of 156 Soviet-assisted construction projects.
13 Xiong (1999), p. 27.
14 Shanghai Municipal Statistics Bureau (1988), p. 80.
15 These statistics appear in the China National Bureau of Statistics (1999), and Shanghai Municipal Statistics Bureau (2011).
16 For views on this see Wang et al. (2010), p. 30.
17 These statistics appear in China National Bureau of Statistics (1999).
18 Enright, Scott and Chang (2005); Shanghai Municipal Statistics Bureau (2011).
19 See http://www.aljazeera.com/news/asia-pacific/2011/12/

2011121463225690525.html [Accessed 9 November 2013].

20  See http://www.chinadaily.com.cn/china/2009-11/05/content_
8915177.htm [Accessed 9 November 2013].

21  The main goals of the CEPA are, in light of the principle 'One country, two systems', to eliminate trade barriers and discriminatory measures, to promote bilateral trade liberalization and cooperation in order to achieve mutual benefit and sustainable development.

22  The data are to be found in Hong Kong SAR Census and Statistics Department at
http://www.censtatd.gov.hk/gb/?param=b5uniS&url=http://www.cen statd.gov.hk/hong_kong_statistics/key_economic_and_social_indica-tors/index_tc.jsp#ext_trade and http://www.stats-sh.gov.cn/data/ release.xhtml [Accessed 9 November 2013] and ShanghaiMunicipal Statistics Bureau (2011).

23  This policy, jointly developed by the People's Bank of China, the Ministry of Finance, the Ministry of Commerce, the General Administration of Customs, the State Administration of Taxes, and the China Banking Regulatory Commission, went into effect on 1 July 2009. Its aims are to promote trade facilitation and cross-border RMB settlement under conditions of controlled risk. See http://www.pbc.gov.cn/publish/huobizhengceersi/3131/2010/201009 15161805939380862/20100915161805939380862.html [Accessed 9 November 2013].

24  Cheung et al. (2011).

25  Chapman et al. (2010), *passim.*

26  For an overview of port facilities, see Cullinane, Wang and Cullinane (2004). For up-to-date port rankings, see http://www.mardep. gov.hk/en/publication/pdf/portstat_2_y_b5.pdf [Accessed 9 November 2013].

27  Wu (2000).

28  Yao et al. (2003), pp. 58–61.

29  Yao (1990) gives a detailed comparison of the differences between the tax rates and tax systems in the two cities. For example, in 1988 Shanghai set the joint-venture tax rate at 30 per cent, the local surtax at 10 per cent, and a combined tax rate of 33 per cent; by comparison, Hong Kong's corporate tax was just 17 per cent. In 2011 a considerable gap still prevailed, with a 25 per cent corporate income tax for most Shanghai enterprises, while Hong Kong's was a mere 16.5 per cent.

30  Guo et al. (2008), pp. 71–74.

31  Lardy (2010).

32  Reference material on US government controls on US financial institutions includes You (2010) and US Department of the Treasury (2009).

33 http://www.wto.org/english/tratop_e/tpr_e/s241_sum_e.pdf [Accessed 9 November 2013]; http://www.forbes.com/lists/2011/6/best-countries-11_Hong-Kong_CHI011.html [Accessed 9 November 2013].

34 You (2010).

35 See the State Council's *Approval of the Shanghai Urban Master Plan* (2001, In Chinese) at: http://www.gov.cn/gongbao/content/2001/content_60877.htm [Accessed 9 November 2013].

36 For reference material on the content of this section, see You Anshan (2010) and Hong Kong Monetary Authority (2010) at http://www.hkma.gov.hk/gb_chi/key-functions/monetary-stability.shtml [Accessed 9 November 2013].

37 See Chen (2010), pp. 91–95.

38 United Nations (2009).

39 Leung and Unteroberdoerster (2008).

40 *Hong Kong Yearbook* (in Chinese, 2011).

41 In 2010 the Yangtze River Delta claimed 121 of China's top 500 enterprises, the Pearl River Delta only 34. The number of Yangtze River Delta enterprises among the top 500 continues to rise while the Pearl River Delta's continue to fall.

42 Data on direct and indirect financial channels may be found on the People's Bank of China website at http://www.pbc.gov.cn/publish/html/2011s01.htm [Accessed 9 November 2013]. For Hong Kong, on the IMF website at http://www.imf.org/eternal/data.htm [Accessed 9 November 2013].

43 See Chen (2006, pp. 33–40) and Morck et al. (2000, pp. 215–260). Morck et al. hold that one method of measuring financial market efficiency is to judge the degree of harmonization in stock price movement; if the market price is able to efficiently reflect all publicly available information then the investor can make a reasonable decision on individual stock based on public information, and by means of this make an individualized investment decision. Therefore, the share price in an efficient market will reflect a share's individual characteristics but will not create a bandwagon effect on the stock market.

44 Burdekin et al. (2008).

45 Zhang et al. (2006), 33–40.

46 Kuilman and Li (2006).

47 See http://www.censtatd.gov.hk/FileManager/EN/ Content_941/06bc_hhinc_slides.pdf [Accessed 9 November 2013]

48 Shanghai Statistics Government Experts' Web Forum (2011).

49 See http://www.hkss.org.hk/SPC/2011-12/AwardPDF/S11-12-DP4.pdf [Accessed 9 November 2013]

50 Wong et al. (2002).

51 Siu and Ku (2008).

# Bibliography

*All about Shanghai and Environs: A Standard Guide Book*. 1935. Shanghai: University Press.

Baark, E. and So, A. Y. 2006. "The Political Economy of Hong Kong's Quest for High Technology Innovation". *Journal of Contemporary Asia* 36.1: 102–120.

Bai, R. 2005. "Media Commercialization, Entertainment, and the Party-state: The Political Economy of Contemporary Chinese Television Entertainment Culture". *Global Media Journal* 4.6: 1–20.

Barber, N. 1979. *The Fall of Shanghai*. New York: Coward, McCann and Geoghegan.

Barraclough, S. 2001. "Satellite Television in Iran: Prohibition, Imitation and Reform". *Middle Eastern Studies* 37.3: 25–48.

Beasley, W.G. 1995. *Great Britain and the Opening of Japan, 1834–1858*. London: Routledge.

Bergère, M.C. 1964. *Une crise financière à shanghai à la fin de l'ancien régime*. Paris: Mouton.

Bergère, M.C. 1981. "The Other China: Shanghai from 1919 to 1949". In Howe, C. ed., *Shanghai: Revolution and Development in an Asian Metropolis*, 1–34. New York: Cambridge University Press.

Bergère, M.C. 1986. *L'Âge d'or de la bourgeoisie chinoise, 1911–1937*. Paris: Flammarion.

Bergère, M.C. 1997."Civil Society and Urban Change in Republican China". *China Quarterly* 150: 309–328.

Bergere, M.C. 2002. *Histoire de Shanghai*. Paris: Fayard.

Bergere, M.C. 2009. *Shanghai: China's Gateway to Modernity*. Stanford, CA: Stanford University Press.

Betta, C. 1997. *Silas Aaron Hardoon (1815–1931): Marginality and Adaptation in Shanghai*. Published PhD Dissertation. London: SOAS.

Bickers, R. 1999a. Book Review of Johnson (1995). *American Historical Review* 102. 2: 499–500.

Bickers, R. 1999b, *Britain in China: Community Culture and Colonialism, 1900–1949*. Manchester: Manchester University Press.

Bickers, R. 2003. *Empire Made Me: An Englishman Adrift in Shanghai*. London: Allen Lane.

Bickers, R. 2007. "Transforming Frank Peasgood: Family Photographs and Shanghai Narratives". *European Journal of East Asian Studies* 6.1: 129–142.

Bickers, R., and Henriot, C. eds. 2000. *New Frontiers: Imperialism's New Communities in East Asia, 1842–1953*. Manchester: Manchester University Press.

Bickers, R., and Wasserstrom, J.N. 1995. "Shanghai's 'Dogs and Chinese not Admitted' Sign: Legend, History and Contemporary Symbol". *China Quarterly* 142: 444–466.

Bowen, J. R., and, Rose, D.C. 1998. "On the Absence of Privately Owned, Publicly Traded Corporations in China: The Kirby Puzzle". *Journal of Asian Studies* 57.2: 442–452.

Brandt, L., and Sargent, T. 1989. "Interpreting New Evidence About China and US Silver Purchases". *Journal of Monetary Economics* 23: 31–51.

Brandt, L. 1989. "Commercialization and Agricultural Development: Central and Eastern China, 1870–1937". New York: Cambridge University Press.

Brook, T. 1990. "Family Continuity and Cultural Hegemony: The Gentry of Ningbo, 1368–1911". In Esherick, J., and Rankin, M.B. eds., *Chinese Local Elites and Patterns of Dominance*, 27–50. Berkeley: University of California Press.

Brown, I. 1989. "Introduction". In idem. ed., *The Economies of Africa and Asia During the Inter-War Depression*, 1–8. London: Routledge.

Burdekin, R., Arquette, G.C., and Brown W.O. 2008. "US ADR and Hong Kong H-Share Discounts of Shanghai-Listed Firms". *Journal of Banking and Finance* 32.9: 1916–1927.

Carroll, J. M. 2007. *A Concise History of Hong Kong*. London: Rowman and Littlefield.

CFHA (China First Historical Archives) comp. 1993. *Select Archival Materials on the Small-Sword Rebellion in Shanghai and Fujian* (in Chinese). Fuzhou: Fujian People's Press.

Chakrabarty, D. 2000. *Provincializing Europe: Postcolonial Thought and Historical Difference*. Princeton: Princeton University Press.

Chang, G.C. 2001. *The Coming Collapse of China*. New York: Random House.

Chapman, D.W., Cummings, W.K., and Postiglione, G.A. eds. 2010. *Crossing Borders in East Asian Higher Education*. New York: Springer.

Chen, C.S. 1965. "Profits of British Bankers from Chinese Loans, 1895–1914". *Tsinghua Journal of Chinese Studies* 5.1: 107–120.

Chen, G. 2008. *Regional Development in China and Pearl River Delta Cooperation* (in Chinese). Guangdong: Sun Yat-sen University Press.

Chen, G. 2009. *A Study of Hong Kong's Restructuring and Development following Its Handover to China* (in Chinese). Beijing: Peking University Press.

Chen, G., Liu, Z., and Yuan, C. 2009. *A Review of Socio-Economic Development in Hong Kong after Its Return to the Mainland* (in Chinese). Guangdong: Sun Yat-sen University Press.

Chen, H. 2010. "A Comparative Analysis of Shanghai and Hong Kong as Global Financial Hubs" (in Chinese). *China Opening Journal* 5: 91–5.

Chen, L., and Zhu, R. 2004. "Examining the Gaps between Shanghai and Hong Kong through Industrial Comparison" (in Chinese). *The Economy of Shanghai and Hong Kong* 3: 38–9.

Chen, Z. 2007. *Looking for Eastern-Ocean Men: Japanese Residents in Modern Shanghai, 1868–1945* (in Chinese). Shanghai: Shanghai Academy of Social Science.

Chen, Z. 2006. "Stock Market in China's Modernization Process – Its Past, Present and Future Prospects". Yale School of Management Working Paper.http://ckgsb.com/web2005/files/forum0607/rhjdzgzqs_chenzhiwu.pdf.

Cheng, L. 2003. *Entrepreneurs, Professional Managers, and the Development of Chinese Banks, 1897–1937*. New York: Cambridge University Press.

Chesneaux, J. 1962. *Le mouvement ouvrier chinois de 1919 a 1927*. Paris: Mouton.

Cheung, P. 1996. "The Political Context of Shanghai's Economic Development". In Yeung, Y.M., and Sung, Y.W, eds., *Shanghai: Transformation and Modernization under China's Open Door*, 49–92. Hong Kong: Chinese University Press.

Cheung, Y., Ma, G., and McCauley, R. 2011. "Renminbising China's Foreign Assets". *Pacific Economic Review* 16.1: 1–17.

China National Bureau of Statistics: Department of Comprehensive Statistics. 1999. *A Compilation of Statistics spanning Five Decades of PRC History* (in Chinese). Beijing: China Statistics Press.

*China's First Modern Bank* (in Chinese). 1982. Compiled by the Institute of Modern History – Chinese Academy of Social Sciences. Beijing: Chinese Academy of Social Sciences.

Chinese Economic Review Publishing Company. 2008. Tales of Old China [Online]. Available: http://www.talesofoldchina.com/

Clark, J.D. 1921. *A Short History of Shanghai*. Shanghai: Shanghai Mercury.

Clifford, N.R. 1991. *Spoilt Children of Empire: Westerners in Shanghai and the Chinese Revolution of the 1920s*. Hanover, NE: University Press of New England.

Coble, P.M. 1980. *The Shanghai Capitalists and the Nationalist Government, 1927–1937*. Cambridge, MA: Harvard University Press.

Coble, P.M. 2003. *Chinese Capitalists in Japan's New Order: the Occupied Lower Yangzi, 1937–1945*. Berkeley: University of California Press.

Cochran, S., ed. 1999. *Inventing Nanjing Road: Commercial Culture in Shanghai, 1900–1945*. Ithaca: Cornell University Press.

Cohen, P. 1984. *Discovering History in China: American Historical Writing on the Recent Chinese Past*. New York: Columbia University Press.

Cullinane, K., Wang , T.F., and Cullinane S. 2004. "Container Terminal Development in Mainland China and Its Impact on the Competitiveness of the Port of Hong Kong". *Transport Reviews: A Transnational Transdisciplinary Journal* 24.1: 33–56.

Cumming, C.F.G. 1886. *Wanderings in China*. Edinburgh: Blackwood.

Dai, A. 1998. *Harbour, City, Hinterland: A Study of the Historic Economic Links between the Lower Yangtze Region and Shanghai, 1843–1913* (in Chinese). Shanghai: Fudan University Press.

Denison, E., and Guan Y.R. 2006. *Building Shanghai: The Story of China's Gateway*. Chichester: Wiley.

Dikötter, F. 2007. *Exotic Commodities: Modern Objects and Everyday Life in China*. New York: Columbia University Press.

Dikötter, F. 2008. *The Age of Openness: China before Mao*. Berkeley: University of California Press.

Dong, D., Jin, W., and Xia, G. 2006. "A Comparative Study of Fluctuations in the Securities Markets of Shanghai, Hong Kong and New York" (in Chinese). *Management Science* 6: 69–74.

Du, X. 2002. *Structral Change and Functionality in Shanghai Finance, 1897–1997* (in Chinese). Shanghai: Shanghai People's Press.

Du, X. 2006. *Customary Law in Early-Modern Shanghai Finance* (in Chinese). Shanghai: Shanghai University of Finance and Economics.

Eastman, Lloyd E. 1974. *The Abortive Revolution : China under Nationalist rule, 1927–1937*. Cambridge, MA: Harvard University Press.

Economist Intelligence Unit. 2008. "Country Profile – China". London: The Economist.

Elvin, M. 1967. *The Gentry Democracy in Shanghai, 1905–1914*. Unpublished PhD Dissertation. University of Cambridge, UK.

Elvin, M. 2008. "Explaining Success: The Transfer of Machine-Making Technology to China before 1937". London School of Economics – Lecture Notes.

Enright, M.J., Scott, E.E., and Chang, K. 2005. *Regional Powerhouse: The Greater Pearl River Delta and the Rise of China*. London: John Wiley & Sons.

Esarey, A. 2005. "Concerning the Market: State Strategies for Controlling China's Commercial Media". *Asian Perspective* 29.4: 37–83

Esherick, J., ed. 2002. *Remaking the Chinese City: Modernity and National Identity, 1900–1950*. Honolulu: University of Hawai'i Press.

Fairbank, J.K. 1953. *Trade and Diplomacy on the China Coast: The Opening of the Treaty Ports, 1842–1854*. Cambridge, MA: Harvard University Press.

Fang S. 1972. *The Small-Sword Rebellion in Shanghai* (in Chinese). Shanghai: Shanghai People's Press.

Farrer, J. 2008. "From 'Passports' to 'Joint Ventures': Intermarriage between Chinese Nationals and Western Expatriates Residing in Shanghai". *Asian Studies Review* 32.1: 7–29.

Faure, D. 2003. *Colonialism and the Hong Kong Mentality*. Hong Kong: Centre of Asian Studies, University of Hong Kong.

Faure, D. 2006. *China and Capitalism: A History of Business Enterprise in Modern China*. Hong Kong: Hong Kong University Press.

Faure, D. and Lee, P.T., eds. 2004. *A Documentary History of Hong Kong*, vol 3. *Economy*. Hong Kong: Hong Kong University Press.

Fewsmith, J. 1985. *Party, State, and Local Elites in Republican China: Merchant Organizations and Politics in Shanghai, 1890–1930*. Honolulu: University of Hawaii Press.

*Finance in Old Shanghai* (in Chinese). 1988. Compiled by Greater Shanghai Municipality. Shanghai: Shanghai People's Press.

Finnane, A., ed. 1999. *Far from Where?: Jewish Journeys from Shanghai to Australia*. Melbourne: Melbourne University Press.

Fogel, J.A. 2000. "'Shanghai-Japan': The Japanese Residents' Association of Shanghai". *Journal of Asian Studies* 59.4: 927–950.

Friedman, M. 1992. "Franklin D. Roosevelt, Silver, and China". *Journal of Political Economy* 100.1: 62–83.

Friedman, M. and Schwartz, A.J. 1963. *A Monetary History of the United States, 1867–1960*. Princeton: Princeton University Press.

Gamble, J. 2003. *Shanghai in Transition: Changing Perspectives and Social Contours of a Chinese Metropolis*. London: Routledge.

Goetzmann, W., Ukhov, A.D., and Zhu, N. 2007. "China and the World Financial Markets 1870–1939: Modern Lessons from Historical Globalization". *Economic History Review* 60.2: 267–312.

Goodman, B. 1995. *Native Place, City, and Nation: Regional Networks and Identities in Shanghai, 1853–1937*. Berkeley: University of California Press.

Goodman, B. 2000a. "The Politics of Representation in 1918 Shanghai". *Harvard Journal of Asiatic Studies* 60. 1: 45–88.

Goodman, B. 2000b. "Improvisations on a Semicolonial Theme, or, How to Read a Celebration of Transnational Urban Community". *Journal of Asian Studies* 59.4: 889–926.

Goodman, B. 2005. "Unvirtuous Exchanges: Women and the Corruptions of the Shanghai Stock Market in the Early Republican Era". In Leutner, M., and Spakowskieds, N., eds. *Women in China: the Republican Period in Historical Perspective*, 551–575. Münster: Lit Verlag.

Goodman, B. 2009. "Questions of Colonialism, Nationalism, and the Early Shanghai Stockmarket" (in Chinese). *Provincial China* 1.1:1–21.

Gui, S., and, Li, R. 2002. *A Comparative Study of Social Policy in Shanghai and Hong Kong* (in Chinese). Shanghai: East China Normal University Press.

Guo, X. 2008. "A Comparative Study of the Service Industry Architecture in Hong Kong and Shanghai" (in Chinese). *Bridge of the Century* 6: 71–4

Gützlaff, K. 1833. *The Journal of Two Voyages along the Coast of China in 1831–1832*. New York: J.P. Haven.

Hao, Y.P. 1970. *The Comprador in Nineteenth Century China: A Bridge Between East and West*. Cambridge, MA: Harvard University Press.

Hao, Y.P. 1986. *The Commercial Revolution in Nineteenth-century China*. Berkeley: University of California Press.

Harwit, E. 2005. "Telecommunications and the Internet in Shanghai: Political and Economic Factors Shaping the Network in a Chinese City". *Urban Studies* 42.10: 1837–1858.

Hausman, W. J., Hertner, P., and Wilkins, M. 2008. *Global Electrification: Multinational Enterprise and International Finance in the History of Light and Power, 1878–2007*. New York: Cambridge University Press.

He, S. 2007. "State-Sponsored Gentrification Under Market Transition: The Case of Shanghai". *Urban Affairs Review* 43.2: 171–198.

Hendrischke, H., and Feng, C., eds. 1999. *The Political Economy of China's Provinces: Comparative and Competitive Advantage*. New York: Routledge.

Henriot, C. 1993. *Shanghai, 1927–1937: Municipal Power, Locality, and Modernization*. Berkeley: University of California Press.

Henriot, C. 2001. *Prostitution and Sexuality in Shanghai: a Social History 1849–1949*. Cambridge: Cambridge University Press.

Henriot, C. 2009. "The Colonial Space of Death in Shanghai" (in Chinese). *Provincial China* (e-journal) 1.1: 1–22

Henriot, C., Cheng, T.E., Barge, O., and Caquard, S. 1999. *Atlas de Shanghai: espaces et représentations de 1849 à nos jours*. Paris: CNRS.

Hershatter, G. 1997. *Dangerous Pleasures: Prostitution and Modernity in Twentieth-century Shanghai*. Berkeley: University of California Press.

*Historic Materials from the Bank of Communications* (in Chinese). 1995. Compiled by State Archive no. 2. Beijing: Financial Press.

*History of the Bank of China's Shanghai Branch* (in Chinese). 1991. Beijing: Economic and Scientific Press.

Hong Kong Monetary Authority. 2011. *Yearbook 2010* (in Chinese). Retrieved from http://www.hkma.gov.hk/gb_chi/publications-and-research/annual-report/2010.shtml.

Hong, J. 1989. *Financial Markets in Modern Shanghai* (in Chinese). Shanghai: Shanghai People's Press.

Hong, Y. 2007. *Studies of Tabloids and Civil Society in Modern Shanghai, 1897–1937* (in Chinese). Shanghai: Shanghai shudian.

Honig, E. 1986. *Sisters and Strangers: Women in the Shanghai Cotton Mills, 1919–1949*. Stanford: Stanford University Press.

Horesh, N. 2009. "Location Is (Not) Everything: Re-Assessing Shanghai's Rise, 1840s -1860s". *Provincial China* 1.2: 61–75.

Howe, C. 1981. "Industrialisation under Conditions of Long-run Population Stability: Shanghai's Achievement and Prospect". In: Howe, C., ed. *Shanghai: Revolution and Development in an Asian Metropolis*, 153–187. Cambridge: Cambridge University Press.

Huang, Y. 2008. *Capitalism with Chinese Characteristics: Entrepreneurship and the State*. Cambridge, UK: Cambridge University Press.

Ishii, K. 2002. "British-Japanese Rivalry in Trading and Banking". In Hunter, J.E., and Sugiyama, S. eds. *The History of Anglo-Japanese Relations, 1600–2000* [vol. 4: *Economic and Business Relations*], 110–132. Basingstoke: Macmillan.

Ji, Z. 2002. *A History of Modern Shanghai Banking: the Rise and Decline of China's Finance Capitalism*. Armonk: M.E. Sharpe.

Johnson, L. 1995. *Shanghai: From Market Town to Treaty Port, 1074–1858*. Stanford: Stanford University Press.

Johnstone, W.C. 1937 [Rep. 1973]. *The Shanghai Problem*. Westport, CN: Hyperion Press.

Jones, S. 1974. "The Ningpo Bang and Financial Power at Shanghai". In Elvin, M. and Skinner, G.W., eds., *The Chinese City Between Two Worlds*, 73–96. Stanford: Stanford University Press.

Jones, S. 1976. "Merchant Investment, Commercialization, and Social Change in the Ningpo Area". In Cohen, P., and Schrecker, J.E., eds. *Reform in Nineteenth Century China*, 41–48. Cambridge, MA: Harvard University Press.

Judge, J. 1996. *Print and Politics: Shibao and the Culture of Reform in Late Qing China*. Stanford: Stanford University Press.

Keane, M. 2009. "The Capital Complex: Beijing's New Creative Clusters". In O'Connor, J. and Kong, L. eds. *Creative Economies, Creative Cities: Asian-European Perspectives*, 77–95. London: Springer.

King, F.H.H. 1965. *A Research Guide to China-Coast Newspapers, 1822–1911*. Cambridge, MA: Harvard University Press.

Kirby, W.C. 1995. "China Unincorporated: Company Law and Business Enterprise in Twentieth-Century China." *Journal of Asian Studies* 54.1: 43–63.

Knight, D.S. 2003. "Shanghai Cosmopolitan: Class, Gender and Cultural Citizenship in Wei Hui's Shanghai Babe". *Journal of Contemporary China* 12.37: 639–653.

Kotenev, A.M. 1925 [Rep. 1968]. *Shanghai: Its Mixed Court and Council*. Taipei: Ch'eng-Wen.

Kowallis, von, J.E.. 2009. "Re-reading Lu Xun in the Shadow of the Beijing Olympics". Paper Presented to the Conference of the Society of Chinese Studies Association of Australia.

Kuilman,. 2007. "Institutional Change, Diversity and Competition: Foreign Banks in Shanghai, 1847–2004". In Krug, B., and

Hendrischke, H. eds. *The Chinese Economy in the 21st Century: Enterprise and Business Behaviour*, 21–41. Cheltenham: Edward Elgar.

Kuilman, J., and Li, J. 2006. "The Organizers' Ecology: An Empirical Study of Foreign Banks in Shanghai". *Organisation Science* 17.3: 385–401.

Lai, H.C., Chiu, Y.C., and Leu, H.D.. 2005. "Innovation Capacity Comparison of China's Information Technology Industrial Clusters: The Case of Shanghai, Kunshan, Shenzhen and Dongguan". *Technology Analysis and Strategic Management* 17. 3: 293–315.

Laing, E.J. 2004. *Selling Happiness: Calendar Posters and Visual Culture in Early-twentieth-century Shanghai*. Honolulu: University of Hawaii Press.

Lardy, N. 2010. *Sustaining China's Economic Growth after the Global Financial Crisis*. Washington, D.C.: Peterson Institute.

Lee, C.C., Zhou, H., and Yu, H. 2007. "Party-Market Corporatism, Clientalism, and Media in Shanghai". *The Harvard International Journal of Press/Politics* 2007: 21–42.

Lee, L.O. 2001. *Shanghai Modern: The Flowering of New Urban Culture in China*. Cambridge, MA: Harvard University Press.

Lee, T.V. 1990. *Law and Local Autonomy at the International Mixed Court of Shanghai*. Unpublished PhD Dissertation. Yale University.

Lee, T.V. 1996. *Coping with Shanghai: Means to Survival and Success in the Early Twentieth Century – A Symposium Introduction. Journal of Asian Studies* 54.1: 3–18.

Leung, C., and Unteroberdoerster, O. 2008. *Hong Kong SAR as a Financial Center for Asia: Trends and Implications*. Washington, D.C.: International Monetary Fund.

Lieu, D. K. 1929. *Foreign Investments in China*. Nanjing: Chinese Government Bureau of Statistics.

Lin, W.Y. 1936. *The New Monetary System of China: a Personal Interpretation*. Shanghai: Kelly and Walsh.

Lindsay, H.H. 1834. *Report of Proceedings on a Voyage to the Northern Ports of China in the Ship Lord Amherst*. London: B. Fellowes.

Liu, S. 1997. "A Centennial Overview of Hong Kong's Political and Economic Evolution" (in Chinese). *Urban Planning and Regulation* 7: 28–31.

Liu, Y. 2006. *The Kincheng Bank* (in Chinese). Beijing: Chinese Academy of Social Sciences.

Liu, Z. 2004. *The Chinese-Run Securities Markets in Pre-War Shanghai* (in Chinese). Shanghai: Xuelin Press.

Liu, H., and Stapleton, K. 2006. *Chinese Urban History: State of the Field. China Information* 20.3: 391–427.

Liu, H., ed. 1985–1987. *History of Modern Shanghai* (in Chinese). Shanghai: East China Normal University Press.

Lu, H. 1992. "Arrested Development: Cotton and Cotton Markets in Shanghai, 1350–1843". *Modern China* 18.4: 468–499.

Lu, H. 1998. "Immigration, Urban-Rural Ties, Culture, Modernization"(in Chinese). In Zhang, Z. ed., *Enterprise, Society and Space in China's Early-Modern Cities* (in Chinese), 392–410. Shanghai: Shanghai Academy of Social Sciences.

Lu, H. 1999. *Beyond the Neon Lights: Everyday Shanghai in the Early Twentieth Century*. Berkeley: University of California Press.

Lui, T.L., and Chiu, S.W.K. 2009. "Becoming a Chinese Global City: Hong Kong (and Shanghai) beyond the Global-Local Duality". In Chen, X. ed. *Shanghai Rising: State Power and Local Transformations in a Global Megacity*, 93–124. Minneapolis: University of Minnesota Press.

Ma, D. 2004. "Growth, Institutions and Knowledge: a Review and Reflection on the Historiography of 18th–20th Century China". *Australian Economic History Review* 44.3: 259–277.

Ma, D. 2005. "Economic Growth in the Lower Yangtze Region of China in 1911–1937: A Quantitative and Historical Analysis. *Journal of Economic History* 68.2: 355–392.

Ma, Z. 2001. "Preliminary Survey of Shanghai International Arrivals and Departures" (in Chinese). *Journal of Shanghai Public Security Academy* 11.3: 42–45.

*Machine-Manufacturing Entrepreneurship in Pre-War Shanghai* (in Chinese), 1979. Compiled by the Shanghai Bureau of Industrial and Commercial Administration. Beijing: Zhonghua shuju.

MacPherson, K.L. 1987. *A Wilderness of Marshes: The Origins of Public Health in Shanghai, 1843–1893*. Hong Kong: Oxford University Press.

MacPherson, K.L. 1996. "The Shanghai Model in Historical Perspective". In Yeung, Y.M. and Sung, Y. eds. *Shanghai: Transformation and Modernization under China's Open Door*, 493–527. Hong Kong: Chinese University Press.

Mak, G.C.L., and Lo, L.N.K. 1996. "Education". In Yeung, Y.M. and Sung, Y. eds. *Shanghai: Transformation and Modernization under China's Open Door*, 375–398. Hong Kong: Chinese University Press.

Mao, D. [Rep. 1957]. *Midnight*. Beijing: Foreign Languages Press.

Mao, G., and Higano, Y. 1996. "A Study of the Labor Input in Shanghai: Effects of Information Development and Employment Policy". *Hitotsubashi Journal of Economics* 37: 155–173.

Martin, B. 1996. *The Shanghai Green Gang: Politics and Organized Crime, 1919–1937*. Berkeley: University of California Press.

McElderry, A.L. 1976. *Shanghai Old-style Banks (Ch'ien-Chuang), 1800–1925: a Traditional Institution in a Changing Society*. Ann Arbor: University of Michigan Press.

McElderry, A.L. 2001. *Shanghai Securities Exchanges: Past and Present*. Brisbane: University of Queensland Working Paper.

Medhurst, W.H. 1838. *China: Its State and Prospects*. London: Crocker & Brewster.

Meng, Y. 2006. *Shanghai and the Edges of Empires*. Minneapolis: University of Minnesota Press.

Menzel, U. 2006. *Sytematische Bibliographie* [Online]. Available: www.tubraunschweig.de/~umenzel/inhalt/dienstleistungen/shanghai.P DF

Meyer, M.J. 2003. *From the Rivers of Babylon to the Whangpoo: A Century of Sephardi Jewish Life in Shanghai*. Lanham: University Press of America.

Miller, M.B. 1994. *Shanghai on the Metro: Spies, Intrigue, and the French between the Wars*. Berkeley: University of California Press.

Minami, R. 1994. *The Economic Development of China: A Comparison with the Japanese Experience*. London: Macmillan.

Miners, N. 1987. *Hong Kong Under Imperial Rule, 1912–1941*. Hong Kong: Oxford University Press.

Mittler, B. 2004. *A newspaper for China?: Power, Identity, and Change in Shanghai's News Media, 1872–1912*. Cambridge, Mass.: Harvard University Press.

Morck, R., Yeung, B., and Yu, W. 2000. "The Information Content of Stock Markets: Why Do Emerging Markets Have Synchronous Stock Price Movements?" *Journal of Financial Economics* 58.1–2: 215–260

Motono, E. 2000. *Conflict and Cooperation in Sino-British Business, 1860–1911: The Impact of the Pro-British Commercial Network in Shanghai*. Basingstoke: Macmillan.

Murphey, R. 1953. *Shanghai: Key to Modern China*. Cambridge, MA: Harvard University Press.

Murphey, R. 1974. "The Treaty-Ports and China's Modernization". In Elvin, M. and Skinner, G.W., eds., *The Chinese City Between Two Worlds*, 17–71. Stanford: Stanford University Press.

Murphey, R. 1977. *The Outsiders: The Western Experience in India and China*. Ann Arbor: Michigan University Press.

N'Diaye, P., and Ahuja, A. 2012. *Trade and Financial Spillover on Hong Kong SAR from a Downturn in Europe and Mainland China*. Washington, D.C.: International Monetary Fund.

Nishimura, S. 2005. "The Foreign and Native Banks in China: Chop Loans in Shanghai and Hankow before 1914". *Modern Asian Studies* 39.1: 109–132.

Nobutaka, I. 1954. "The Pattern of Railway Development in Japan". *The Far Eastern Quarterly* 14.1: 217–229.

Noda, M. 1980. *History of the Japanese Securities Markets* (in Japanese). Tokyo: Yūhikaku.

O'Connor, J. 2009. "Shanghai Moderne: Creative Economy in a Creative City?" In O'Connoir and Kong, L. eds., *Creative Economies, Creative*

*Cities : Asian-European Perspectives*, 175–193. London, UK: Springer.

Oi, J. C., and Walder, A.G., eds. 1999. *Property Rights and Economic Reform in China*. Stanford: Stanford University Press.

Paauw, D.S. 1950. *Chinese Public Finance During the Nanking Government Period*. Published PhD Dissertation. Harvard University.

Pan, L. 2008. *Shanghai Style: Art and Design Between the Wars*. San Francisco: Long River Press.

Perry, E.J. 1993. *Shanghai on Strike: The Politics of Chinese Labor*. Stanford: Stanford University Press.

Pott, H.F.L. 1928. *Short History of Shanghai: Being an Account of the Growth and Development of the International Settlement*. Shanghai: Kelly and Walsh.

Qian, Y. 2002. "How the Reform Worked in China". University of California, Department of Economics; Centre for Economic Policy Research (CEPR). William Davidson Institute Working Paper Number 473.

Raiser, S. , and Volkmann, K. 2007. "Conclusion". In Segbers, K. ed., *The Making of Global City Regions: Johannesburg, Mumbai/Bombay, São Paulo, and Shanghai*, 339–355. Baltimore: Johns Hopkins University Press.

Rankin, M.B. 1986. *Elite Activism and Political Transformation in China, Zhejiang Province 1865–1911*. Stanford: Stanford University Press.

Rawski, T. 1989. *Economic Growth in Prewar China*. Berkeley: University of California Press.

Rawski, T. 1993. "Milton Friedman, Silver, and China". *Journal of Political Economy* 101.4: 755–758.

Reed, C. 2004. *Gutenberg in Shanghai: Chinese Print Capitalism, 1876–1937*. Honolulu: University of Hawaii Press.

*Reprints of the Minutes of the SMC Executive Committee* (in Chinese). 2001. Shanghai: Shanghai Municipal Archives.

Rigby, R.W. 1980. *The May 30 Movement: Events and Themes*. Canberra: Australian National University Press.

Ristaino, M.R. 2001. *Port of Last Resort: The Diaspora Communities of Shanghai*. Stanford: Stanford University Press.

Rogaski, R. 2004. *Hygienic Modernity: Meanings of Health and Disease in Treaty-Port China*. Berkeley: University of California Press.

Roux, A. 1993. *Le Shanghai ouvrier des années trente: coolies, gangsters et syndicalistes*. Paris: L'Harmattan.

Rowe, P.G., and Kuan, S. eds. 2004. *Shanghai: Architecture and Urbanism for Modern China*. Munich: Prestel Verlag.

Rowe, W.T. 1984. *Hankow: Commerce and Society in a Chinese City, 1796–1889*. Stanford: Stanford University Press.

Rowe, W.T. 2010. *China's Last Empire: The Great Qing*. Cambridge, MA: Harvard University Press.

*Rubber-Industry Entrepreneurship in Pre-War Shanghai* (in Chinese). 1979. Comp. by the Shanghai Bureau of Industrial and Commercial Administration. Beijing: Zhonghua shuju.

Schenk, C. 2007. *Hong Kong as an International Financial Centre: Emergence and Development, 1945–1965.* London: Routledge.

Shanghai Economists' Association. 1992. *Development, Opening Up, Liberalisation: A Comprehensive Overview of Shanghai's Development* (in Chinese). Beijing: China Radio and Television Press.

Shanghai Municipal Statistics Bureau. 1988. *Shanghai: Reform, Opening Up, and Development* (in Chinese). Shanghai: SDX Joint Publishing Company.

Shanghai Municipal Statistics Bureau. 2011. *Shanghai Statistical Yearbook 2010* (in Chinese).

Shanghai Statistics Government Experts' Web Forum. 2011. "The Kuznets Curve Cannot Explain China's Income Inequalities" (in Chinese). Retrieved from http://www.stats-sh.gov.cn/tjqt/201105/220302.html.

Sheehan, B.. 2003. Review of Cheng (2003). *Business History Review* 77.4: 811–813.

Shelp, R. 2006. *Fallen Giant: The Amazing Story of Hank Greenberg and the History of AIG.* Hoboken, NJ: Wiley.

Shiroyama, T. *China during the Great Depression: Market, State, and the World Economy, 1929–1937.* Cambridge, Mass.: Harvard University Press.

Siu, H.F., and Ku, A.S.M. 2008. *Hong Kong Mobile: Making a Global Population.* Hong Kong: Hong Kong University Press.

Stephens, T.B. 1992. *Order and Discipline in China: The Shanghai Mixed Court, 1911–27.* Seattle: University of Washington Press.

Strand, D. 1989. *Rikshaw Beijing: City People and Politics in the 1920s.* Berkeley: University of California Press.

Sun, S. 1990. *A Study of Newly-Found Historic Materials on the Small Sword Rebellion* (in Chinese). Shenyang: Liaoning University Press.

Swislocki, M. 2009. *Culinary Nostalgia: Regional Food Culture and the Urban Experience in Shanghai.* Stanford: Stanford University Press.

Takatsuna, H. 2009. *Global Metropolis: Japanese Expatriates in Pre-War Shanghai* (in Japanese). Tokyo: Kenpun Press.

Tang, Z. 1989. *History of Shanghai* (in Chinese), Shanghai: Shanghai People's Press.

Tang, Z., ed. 1989. *Chronology of Modern Shanghai* (in Chinese). Shanghai: Cishu Press.

Thomas, S.C. 1984. *Foreign Intervention and China's Industrial Development, 1870–1911.* Boulder, CL: Westview Press.

Thomas, W.A. 2001. *Western Capitalism in China: A History of the Shanghai Stock Exchange.* Aldershot: Ashgate.

Thomas, W.A. 2001, Western Capitalism in China: A History of the Shanghai Stock Exchange, Ashgate, Burlington.

Tsai, K.S. 2007. *Capitalism Without Democracy: The Private Sector in Contemporary China*. Ithaca: Cornell University Press.

Tsang, S. 2007. *A Modern History of Hong Kong*. London: Tauris.

United Nations. 2009. *Harmonious Cities: A Report on the State of World Cities* (in Chinese). Beijing: China Construction Industry Press.

Urmston, J.B. 1834. *Observations on the China Trade and the Importance of Removing from Canton*. London: Baily & Co.

US Department of the Treasury. 2009. *Financial Regulatory Reform – A new Foundation: Rebuilding Financial Supervision and Regulation*. Retrieved from www.treasury.gov/initiatives/Documents/Final Report_web.pdf

Wagner, R.G. 1995, "The Role of the Foreign Community in the Chinese Public Sphere". *China Quarterly* 142: 423–443.

Wagner, R.G. 1999. "The Shenbao in Crisis: the International Environment and the Conflict between Guo Songtao and the Shenbao". *Late Imperial China* 20.1: 107–138.

Wakeman, F. 1993. "The Civil Society and Public Sphere Debate: Western Reflections on Chinese Political Culture". *Modern China* 19. 2: 108–138.

Wakeman, F. 1995. *Policing Shanghai, 1927–1937*. Berkeley: University of California Press.

Wakeman, F., and Edmonds, R.L., eds. 2000. *Reappraising Republican China*. New York: Oxford University Press.

Waldron, A. 1995. *From War to Nationalism: China's Turning Point, 1924–1925*. Cambridge: Cambridge University Press.

Wang, C. 2007. *Shanghai 1843–1956: The History of Foreign Merchants* (in Chinese), Shanghai: Shanghai Academy of Social Sciences.

Wang, J. 1965. *Ethnic Chinese Shareholders of Foreign Companies Operating in Nineteenth-Century China* (in Chinese). *Historical Research* 4: 39–74.

Wang, J. 2007. "Officialdom Unmasked: Shanghai Tabloid Press, 1897–1911". *Late Imperial China* 28.2: 81–128.

Wang, J. 2008. *A Social History of Jewish Life in Shanghai* (in Chinese). Shanghai: Cishu Press.

Wang, R. 2007. *Imagination of Desire: A Study of Advertisements in Shenbao during the 1920–30s* (in Chinese). Shanghai: Shanghai People's Press.

Wang , Z., ed. 2010. *The Strategy Informing Shanghai's Grooming as a Global Metropolis* (in Chinese). Shanghai: Shanghai People's Press.

Wasserstrom, J.N. 1998. *Student Protests in Twentieth-Century China: The View from Shanghai*. Stanford: Stanford University Press.

Wasserstrom, J.N. 2000. "Locating Old Shanghai: Having Fits about Where It Fits". In Esherick, J.W. ed., *Remaking the Chinese City:*

*Modernity and National Identity, 1900–1950,* 192–210. Honolulu: University of Hawai'i Press.

Wasserstrom, J.N. 2008. "Cosmopolitan Connections and Transnational Networks". In Dillon, N., and Oi, J.C. eds., *At The Crossroads of Empires: Middlemen, Social Networks, and State-Building in Republican Shanghai,* 206–223. Stanford: Stanford University Press.

Wasserstrom, J.N. 2009. *Global Shanghai, 1850–2010: A History in Fragments.* London: Routledge.

Weber, I. 2002. "'Shanghai Baby': Negotiating Youth Self-Identity in Urban China". *Social Identities* 8.2: 347–368.

Wong, S.L. 1988. *Emigrant Entrepreneurs : Shanghai Industrialists in Hong Kong.* New York: Oxford University Press.

Wong, S.L. 1996. "The Entrepreneurial Spirit: Shanghai and Hong Kong Compared". In Yeung, Y.M., and Sung, Y.W. eds., *Shanghai: Transformation and Modernization under China's Open Door,* 25–48. Hong Kong: Chinese University Press.

Wong, C.K., Chau, K.L.M., and Wong, T.K.Y. 2002. "Neither Welfare State nor Welfare Society: The Case of Hong Kong". *Social Policy and Society* 1.4: 293–301.

Wood, F. 1998. *No dogs and Not Many Chinese: Treaty Port Life in China 1843–1943.* London: John Murray.

Wright, A. 1908. *Twentieth Century Impressions of Hongkong, Shanghai, and Other Treaty Ports.* London: Lloyds.

Wu, F. 2000. "The Global and Local Dimensions of Place-making: Remaking Shanghai as a World City". *Urban Studies* 37.8: 1359–1377.

Wu, F. 2007. "From 'State-Owned' to 'City Inc': the Case of Shanghai". In Segbers, K., ed. *The Making of Global City Regions: Johannesburg, Mumbai/Bombay, São Paulo, and Shanghai,* 207–231. Baltimore: Johns Hopkins University Press.

Wu, J., and Ma, C., eds. 2003. *The Modernization and Internationalization of Shanghai Finance* (in Chinese). Shanghiai: Guji Press.

Wu, W. 2004. "Cultural Strategies in Shanghai: Regenerating Cosmopolitanism in an era of Globalization". *Progress in Planning* 61:159–180.

Wu, W. 2007. "Shanghai: The Evolution of China's Future Global City". In Segbers, K., ed. *The Making of Global City Regions: Johannesburg, Mumbai/Bombay, São Paulo, and Shanghai,* 113–134. Baltimore: Johns Hopkins University Press.

Xiong, Y. 1996. "The Image and Identity of the Shanghainese". In Liu, T., and Faure D. eds. *Unity and Diversity: Local Cultures and Identities in China,* 99–106. Hong Kong: Hong Kong University Press.

Xiong, Y. chief ed. 1999. *Comprehensive History of Shanghai* (in Chinese), 12 vols. Shanghai: Shanghai People's Press.

Xiong, Y., and Zhou, W., eds. 2004. *Shanghai Studies around the World* (in Chinese). Shanghai: Guji Press

Xu, B. 2007. *Looking for Jewish Heritage: The Cultural Elites of the Jewish Community in Pre-War Shanghai* (in Chinese). Shanghai: Shanghai Academy of Social Sciences.

Xu, X. 2001. *Chinese Professionals and the Republican State: The Rise of Professional Associations in Shanghai, 1912–1937*. New York: Cambridge University Press.

Yang, M.M.H. 2002. "Mass Media and Transnational Subjectivity in Shanghai: Notes on (Re)Cosmopolitanism in a Chinese Metropolis". In Inda, J.X., and Rosaldo, R. eds., *The Anthropology of Globalization*, 325–349. Malden, MA: Blackwell Publishing.

Yang, X. 2006. *Whipped by Empire, Chained by Oligarchy: a Historic Study of Shanghai's Mixed Court* (in Chinese). Beijing: Peking University Press.

Yao, S., Nian, F., and Chen, Z. 2003. "Shanghai and Hong Kong's Status as World Cities" (in Chinese). *Urban Planning Review* 3: 28–31.

Yao, X. 1990. *A Comparative Study of Shanghai and Hong Kong* (in Chinese). Shanghai: Shanghai People's Press.

Ye, X. 2003. *The Dianshizhai Pictorial: Shanghai Urban Life, 1884–1898*. Ann Arbor: University of Michigan Press.

Yeh, W. 2007. *Shanghai Splendor: Economic Sentiments and the Making of Modern China, 1843–1949*. Berkeley: University of California Press.

Yeung, Y.M. 1996. "Introduction". In Yeung, Y.M., and Sung, Y.W. eds., *Shanghai: Transformation and Modernization under China's Open Door*, 1–23. Hong Kong: Chinese University Press.

Yeung, Y., Sung, E. , and Sung, Y.W., eds. 1996. *Shanghai: Trans-formation and Modernization Under China's Open Policy*. Hong Kong: Chinese University Press.

You, A. 2010. *A Report on Economic Development in Shanghai and Hong Kong 2009–2010* (in Chinese). Shanghai: Shanghai Academy of Social Sciences Press.

Zhang, C., ed. 2005. *The Illustrious History of Shanghai Buildings* (in Chinese). Shanghai: Sanlian Press.

Zhang, N. 1936. *The Monetray and Financial Problems of China* (in Chinese). Shanghai: Shenghuoshudian.

Zhang, Y., Shi, Z., and Chen, Y. 2006. "The Efficacy of Stock Markets in China and Hong Kong" (in Chinese). *Financial Research* 6: 33–40.

Zhang, Z. 1996. *Coastal Cities in the Southeast and Their Contribution to China's Modernisation* (in Chinese). Shanghai: People's Press.

Zheng, Y. 2006. *Shanghai Tempest: Chen Liangyu's Dismissal and the End of the Shanghai Clique* (in Chinese). Hong Kong: Wenhua Yishu Press.

Zhong, X. 2006. "Who Is a Feminist? Understanding the Ambivalence towards Shanghai Baby, 'Body Writing' and Feminism in Post-Women's Liberation China". *Gender & History* 18.3 635–660.

Zhou, J. 2004. *The Subao Case* (in Chinese). Shanghai: Shanghai Academy of Social Sciences.

Zhou, M., and Tang, Z., eds. 1999. *Historic Records of Sino-Foreign Contact in Shanghai* (in Chinese). Shanghai: Shanghai Academy of Social Sciences.

# Index